We're All In This Together:
Not Ordinary Devotions

Opportunities for reflection and action for the healing of Creation
through poetry, prose, and the occasional rant
In other words, a book of (not ordinary) prayer

Allyson Sawtell

Parson's Porch Books

We're All In This Together: Not Ordinary Devotions
ISBN: Softcover 978-1-960326-36-2
Copyright © 2023 by Allyson Sawtell

Parson's Porch Books is an imprint of Parson's Porch *&* Company (PP*&*C) in Cleveland, Tennessee. PP*&*C is a self-funded charity which earns money by publishing books of noted authors, representing all genres. Its face and voice is **David Russell Tullock** who you can contact at: dtullock@parsonsporch.com.

Parson's Porch *&* Company *turns books into bread & milk* by sharing its profits with the poor.

www.parsonsporch.com

We're All In This Together:
Not Ordinary Devotions

Contents

Seasonal

Sending Forth

Introduction

This is a book of meditations that seek to be not-ordinary. We are not living in ordinary times. Why should our religious/spiritual life be ordinary?

These readings are designed to help us, or challenge us, to look at ourselves in a different way, to see the world in a different way, to see our faith (however we define that) in a different way.

These readings are based several premises: 1) Our planet, God's good Creation, is under assault from pollution, desertification, species extinction, climate change, war, social injustice, habitat loss, and on and on. 2) Time is short to rectify the worst of the damage our species has inflicted on our world. 3) How we speak, how we view ourselves in relationship with Creation, how we view the world, will determine how we will live with ourselves, each other, and all Creation. 4) We are called to be a people of hope, which is different from optimism. And we *can* be a people of hope.

These devotions are not always humano-centric. I believe our faith needs to be likewise. Our language needs to be likewise. We share this planet, this life, with air, water, soil, starlight, creatures, and that mysterious "holy" in our midst, which many call God. That force which is founded on and bending towards deep, deep love.

Words matter. This devotional guide is one attempt to speak new words in the hope that change and healing might happen in this good Creation.

And so, who is this for, you might ask?

This devotional guide is for those who are religiously skeptical.
And for the theologically certain.
And for those somewhere in between.

And especially for those who have an irreverent sense of humor.

Those who believe passionately in the vital power of community.
And those who wish to believe so.

For those who are honest with their doubts.

7

And those yet to discover and own those doubts.

For the yearning.

Oh, basically, for put near everyone who might want to try to find meaning in these words for their lives.

Like the Communion Table (in my view), these writings are open to anyone to partake.

I know not everyone will choose to do so.

But God (as-you-understand-him-her-them) bless you every one!

How to use this guide

These writings are meant to serve as opportunities for meditation and/or prayer.

They can be used daily from Page 1 to the end, or in any order you prefer. They are not organized around the calendar year or the church year, except for some seasonal-specific readings.

There is, surprisingly, still a structure to these not-ordinary devotions! Each reading (poem, essay, rant, prayer) is meant to be experienced much like the Lectio Divina (in which the same Scripture passage is read several times in a row, each time focusing on a different aspect). These readings are to be experienced like that, only over a period of 1-3 days. Each reading will have questions, comments, and/or calls to action for you to take on, as well. Or, you could just read one a day and not spread it out.

So, simply, here are some thoughts/prayers/poems/rants for you to work through as you see fit.

Other important information

The pieces in this book were all written by me, although I may make reference to other writers. I have also included links to items of interest for some of the readings.

Some of these pieces may also be found on my website, Not Ordinary Church (https://allyson.revsawtell.org/) All of these readings, as well as the ones on my website (which you really should check out!) can be used royalty-free under the guidelines of the Creative Commons (https://creativecommons.org/licenses/by-nc-nd/4.0/)

I suspect some may be offended by some of these pieces. Too irreverent, too liberal, too religious, too down to earth, too female, too light-hearted, too many dog references and not enough cat references, too serious….

Feel free to own your feelings.

However, even as I try not to make assumptions based on privilege, etc., when the offense is due to my inadvertently or ignorantly living out of my own cluelessness, I am deeply sorry for the hurt I caused, and I promise to continue to work on that. Please let me know.

Thank you for joining in on not-ordinary devotions. May some pieces touch you, cause you to question, think, cry, laugh out loud, or even ask, "What was she thinking??"

Enjoy!

Peace,
Allyson Sawtell (she/hers)

With thanks and love to my proofreaders and beloveds:
Pamela   Scott   Gail   Gaye   Joyce
And, always,
Peter

A Blessing to Begin
A Benediction to Start

Simply read these two readings over a period of a few days. Sit with them. See what feelings, images, thoughts come to your mind. Respond to them.

Then, in the spirit of these blessings, move on through the devotional guide at your own pace.

A Blessing for the Earth

Day One

Bless the Earth, O my soul
Who are we to bless her?
What magnanimous gesture can we bestow upon our Earth?
   A heartfelt plea for Earth's well-being, that goodness will come
   her way?

Yet empty prayers swirl in the disruptive rending and violating
actions of our species.
And hollow prayers strike at her with discordant sound that
reverberates in anguish.

Bless the Earth, O my soul
We are to bless her.
Remove us from words into ways of being and moving.

Step outside of ourselves:
   Outside our ego and its demands for centrality.
And bless the earth from a place of awe and wonder.
   (The ripping, tearing reverberations of destruction are still there,
   make no mistake. But so is awe, and so is beauty. And tiny
   saplings emerging from the ashes)

Day Two

Bless the Earth, O my soul
May you be held in arms of grace
Comforted through acts of courage
Explored with gentleness and curiosity.

May the incredible and miraculous inner workings of your intricate
        web of life
   be strengthened and healed
   the irreparably broken places confessed and lamented
   and accountability and justice be given.

Bless the Earth, O my soul
   and know the lament embedded within.

Bless the Earth, O my soul
Her strength and beauty
Her tears, her vitality
Her growth
Her change

Bless the Earth, O my soul
And us, too – part and parcel of her being – bless us with courage,
action, will, and passion.

Bless the Earth, O my soul

Deep Peace

(Adapted from the Celtic Blessing of the same name)

Day One

Deep peace of the running wave to you.
Swelling, breaking on rock,
exploding in power,
Receding – leaving its legacy in tidal pools and starfish on the
sand.
Life and death.
Power and quietude.

Water. Water that gives us life even in its turbulence.

And connects us to all things.

Deep peace of the running wave break in you and through you and
from you.

Deep peace of the flowing air to you.
Gentle breeze, caress, promise of spring after a harsh winter.
Gentle breeze, with its soft, warm edges.

Turbulent storm, funnel cloud that
swirls around our heads its despair, grief, outrage and injustice.
Threatening destruction, and often making good its threat.

Strong wind blowing away the leaves, the ashes,
the dust that covers up what desperately needs the sunshine.

Air that gives us life, even with its turmoil and questions.

And connects us to all things.

Deep peace of the flowing air breathe in you and through you and
from you.

Day Two

Deep peace of the quiet earth to you.
    Forests and caverns and mountains holding and sheltering life,
    Solid ground beneath our feet,
    Promise of life from rich soil.

Tectonic plates eternally shifting, making and remaking in
          uprooting disruption.
Change at its most vehement.
Volcanic lava eruptions. Pyroclastic flows. Wind-blown wildfires.

And green life peeking through in the aftermath.
The "still, small voice" out of Creation's upheaval.

This is us.
We are of Earth in all its wild dance of death and life,
  of tumult and quiet, of disruption and shelter,

And we are connected to all that is.

Deep peace of the quiet earth dance in you and through you and
          from you.

Deep peace of the shining stars to you.
Ancient, far away light.
Given from stars long dead, or simply old beyond our imaginings.
A gift from the past that seems a promise for the future.

Stars near-eternal, moving with galactic slowness through the
          universe.
A comforting grandeur:
  we are not all that is or ever will be,
but we *are* in this place and in this time, with star-shine our
          inheritance and our legacy.

Stars whirling, burning, exploding, hurtling through space and
          lighting up our sky.
Challenging and enlivening vitality and power, that calls us into the
          dance.
Stars pouring out themselves into vast space, and an unknown
          future.

We are of the same matter as the stars.

And we are connected to all that was and is and is yet to be.

Deep peace of the shining stars burn in you and through you and from you.

Day Three

**Deep peace of the gentle night to you. Moon and stars pour
their healing light on you.**
Interplay of light and dark. A dance, duet, balancing act.

Stars and night and moon: Inexorable pull of tides in oceans and
our own bodies.
The marker of seasons.
Guiding lights, showing paths unknown.
Dark embrace of dreams, rest.

Darkness that can confront us with our fears and call forth our
courage.
Light that can overwhelm us and blind us and awaken us.

Ancient light, ancient darkness.

Blessed darkness hold you and heal you.
Blessed light awaken you and guide you.

Night, moon, stars connect you to all things.

Deep peace of light and dark dance in you and through you and
from you.

*After you've read this piece, you could listen to a recording of the version crafted
by composer John Rutter. Google John Rutter Deep Peace.*

Readings
of
Awe, Lament, Hope, Gratitude, Wondering, Celebration

Read through this section in any order you wish. Read one each day, or each week. Take a day to read, reflect, engage in the suggested activities. Or take a couple of days to do so. Elsewhere in the guide there is a Seasonal section – as you approach certain holidays, you may want to leave this more "generic" section and go to the Seasonal one for a bit.

A Prayer of Praise and of Opening

God of earth and sky, of seas, forests, cities, farms, mountains and meadows, I give thanks for your good Creation, and I celebrate your family of life!

God of stars and planets, of bugs and birds and people and all creatures great and small, I give thanks for your good Creation, and I celebrate your family of life!

Open me up, God to the wonder of your good Creation, its beauty and grace. And even for those parts I may have a hard time with, like wasps, or foxes eating baby rabbits, I still give thanks for cycles of life and offer gratitude for everyone's part in it.

Open me up, God, to gratitude and celebration. Open me up also, O God, to the pain of your good Creation, to the cries of all your children.

Give me courage to feel the grief and outrage, and to work towards justice and healing of all your children.

Open me up, God, to wonder, grief, courage, and gratitude. I give thanks, O God, and I celebrate with you and your whole community of life!

Ongoing Reflection Questions, Suggestions, and/or Things to Think About

- Read/pray this all the way through once and see what parts immediately jump out at you. Make note of that, and reflect on what jumped out at you and why. Did the words touch you? Did you argue with them? How did they make you feel? What action did they call you do to, if any?

- Read this a second time (maybe even a day later). What new thing(s) jumped out at you, and why?

- Read it a third time (maybe another day later). What else jumped out at you? This re-reading of a passage is loosely adapted from the ancient Lectio Divina spiritual practice, a way of reading scripture to delve into its meaning, by reading and going deeper each time.

- Based on this reading and your own reflections, do any scripture passages come to mind? These can be scriptures from a variety of religious traditions.

We Hold These Truths...

We hold these truths to be

(kind of)

 self-evident:

> We are connected to something greater than ourselves
>
> What we are truly based on is…love
>
> We are not creatures alone, but are connected to each other in ways known and unknown
>
> We are not here for ourselves alone
>
> We are here so that we can love each other
>
> "Each other" means all creation *and* that great mystery we've spent millennia trying to name

Ongoing Reflection Questions, Suggestions, and/or Things to Think About

- What's missing, for you, from these "self-evident truths"? Can you write your own, in your own words?

- Take a piece of scratch paper, note paper, or poster paper, and tape it up on your wall. This is your "graffiti" board – each day write a word or two that describes your truth. Or draw a picture, if that comes more easily to you.

- What is one thing you might do to live out these truths? What are you doing already? What do you wish you could do, but something holds you back?

- What do you need from that "great mystery" that many of us call "God"?

- Based on this reading and your own reflections, do any scripture passages come to mind? These can be scriptures from a variety of religious traditions.

For Endangered and Extinct Species

Excerpted and adapted from Blessing of the Animals: A Celebration in Two Parts, https://allyson.revsawtell.org/blessing-of-the-animals-a-celebration-in-two-parts/

When Mother Jones said, "Pray for the dead, and fight like hell for the living," she was not thinking of the West African Black Rhinoceros, the Pinta Giant Tortoise, the Splendid Poison Frog, or the Bramble Cay Mosaic-Tailed Rat. All these gone extinct in the last decade or so.

Nor did Mother Jones specifically call us to fight like hell for the Amur Leopard, three species of Rhino, the Bornean Orangutan, or the African Forest Elephant. All critically endangered.

But shall we, anyway? Pray and fight like hell?

If we wish to bless the wild creatures, and pray for the wild creatures, we will hold space for, and mourn, all those gone extinct. Let there be an empty space in our hearts, so we know the loss deep down. And may grief kindle compassion and hard work.

And we celebrate those brought back from the brink of extinction (like the humpback whale and the greater one-horned rhino). May their light never go out! May their light burn strongly and live! May we find ways to make that so.

Ongoing Reflection Questions, Suggestions, and/or Things to Think About

- Today, whenever you are home, light a candle for hope for endangered and threatened species. Next to it place an unlit candle, to represent those species gone extinct. Make a point throughout your day or evening, or whenever you are home, to stop in front of this small, makeshift altar. Pause, reflect, feel, think.

- And celebrate in your heart the critters brought back from extinction. Offer gratitude for all those working so hard to save them.

- Zoos often come under criticism for keeping animals in captivity. And while some zoos are way worse at taking care of their animals, others have created appropriate habitat for their animals and participate in conservation programs that have been instrumental in bringing animals back from extinction. Research your local zoo. If they're doing good work, thank them for it. Maybe even volunteer! If they're not, look into what activism is going on in your community to fight that animal abuse.

- Based on this reading and your own reflections, do any scripture passages come to mind? These can be scriptures from a variety of religious traditions.

So, Here You Are

Originally a Call to Worship, you can read this, by yourself, in your own private devotions, knowing that you are part of a greater community. Whether it is a faith community, a family, Creation's Web of Life, or the folks in your co-housing situation, all of that can be sacred ground. In your heart and mind, stand on that holy ground as you read this prayer.

O God, here I am, in a space made sacred by the power of love
        and community. Here I am.
But who am I, actually, who stands on this holy ground?

Am I Consumer? Controller? Helpless, fearful, disempowered? Am I lover, hope-bearer, seeker? Ordinary person of spirit, energy, and beauty?

So I repeat, who am I who stands on holy ground??

I am a child of God, called to redefine myself as one within the community of all life, sharing sacred space with all your beloved children of all species and types.

So don't let me forget that, O God. In my work and worship, in my life outside my community, don't let me forget that we are all connected. That we are, in truth, one body, connected in the web of life.

So, here I am. In a space made sacred by the power of love and community. Put me to work!

Ongoing Reflection Questions, Suggestions, and/or Things to Think About

- What are the sacred spaces for you? What is your community? You probably have more than one. Just breathe, take a moment, and sit with wonder, awe, and gratitude for the power of community.

- Spend some time listening to the Wailin' Jennys song "One Voice". You can Google Wailin' Jennys One Voice. And while they sing about "one people" and not "one creation", it's still a good song.

- And here are the lyrics –

  https://www.azlyrics.com/lyrics/wailinjennys/onevoice.html

- Based on this reading and your own reflections, do any scripture passages come to mind? These can be scriptures from a variety of religious traditions.

Making Sense

What is the color of anxiety?

                                        What is the touch of a sunset?

        How does hope taste?

                                            What is the sound of fear?

What is the shape of joy?

Ongoing Reflection Questions, Suggestions, and/or Things to Think About

- We don't usually think about hope having a flavor, or joy taking a particular shape, and so on. Done this way, these images/phrases can help stretch our exploration of hope, or joy, or to see/experience them in a different way.

- Write your responses to these questions. Take a couple of days to do this, if you want.

- Write your own questions in this manner. Maybe share them with another.

- Based on this reading and your own reflections, do any scripture passages come to mind? These can be scriptures from a variety of religious traditions.

Falling in Love with Creation

Falling in love with Creation means falling in love with
    ourselves
    each other
    our neighbor
And who is our neighbor?

Draw the circle wide. What does it include?
Who sits with you at the table? And whose table is it? Just yours?
       Or a co-creation?
Do you join hands – and paws – and wing – and rock – and waves?
    Or just hands?

Who is our neighbor?
    The guy next door with the loud stereo?
    The hive of bees across the street?
    The family boarding the bus to head north to new life new
language new home? New cages?

Draw the circle wide.

Who do you love? How do you love?

Is love a feeling? A decision? An act of will?

We do not stand outside of the Creation we love;
    there is no "out there" out there.

Ongoing Reflection Questions, Suggestions, and/or Things to Think About

- We are all part of the web of life; we are all connected.

- Draw a large circle. Drawing or writing (or cutting pictures out of magazines), put in the circle the ones you would identify as in your circle. Who is outside your circle? Who makes you uncomfortable? Who do you know needs to be in the circle, but you'd rather not put them there (in other words, who are we called to love that we don't really like)?

- Reflect on the difference between "circle" and "bubble" (as in, we so often live in our own "bubbles.")

- There is a rather hilarious YouTube video by Clarke and Dawe, an Australian satire news television program that was aired in Australia in the 1990s (To watch, just Google "the front fell off"). The "interview" talks about a tanker that spilled thousands of tons of crude oil into the ocean near Western Australia, because "the front fell off." But not to worry, the spokesperson says, they towed the tanker "outside of the environment", where there's nothing out there but just sea, birds, and fish. The obvious question is, "What's wrong with this picture?" If you need a laugh while reacting to hard stuff, this one might be fun and is somewhat related to our reading! In fact, it inspired the last line.

- Based on this reading and your own reflections, do any scripture passages come to mind? These can be scriptures from a variety of religious traditions.

The Silence Between the Notes

We are the silence between the notes.
We're not the Amen.

We're the waiting, the leaning forward,
        the yearning push to the next sound.

There is something deeper in that space between the notes,
        something infinite, a breath of air.
Anticipation.

Shimmering reverberations of music left behind,
        and anticipatory echoes of what will be.

What is faith? What is hope?

What is found in the silence between the notes?

Ongoing Reflection Questions, Suggestions, and/or Things to Think About

- A musician friend of mine often talked of the silence between the notes. Does that make any sense to you? That anticipatory space. That space of rest.

- I've also discovered that if you listen closely enough, there's a quality of aliveness to the silence. One of my favorite pieces to listen to in this context is Bobby McFerrin's rendition of The 23rd Psalm, from his *Medicine Music* album. If you can find that, give it a listen. What does the silence feel like to you? Or, listen to your own favorite music – and its silences.

- If you simply can't stand music, then you may not want to spend a lot of time on this reading, and that's fine! Think about silence, though, and its vibrant quality.

- Based on this reading and your own reflections, do any scripture passages come to mind? These can be scriptures from a variety of religious traditions.

Dark-Light Times

These are dark times
    Times that repel light – That swallow light – That obscure the
        path – That shelter the unknown
    That make us frightened.

These are dark times
    Times of rich, deep, black soil where seeds once thought dead
        begin to rise up
    Where new seeds incubate in nurturing darkness, drinking in the
        power
    Where courage embraces the unknown
    Where we can be sheltered for a time.
Glossy midnight black shining with stars

These are light times
    Times of searing whiteness that blots out all other colors,
        blistering and scorching as it declares its power, and that
        burns the emerging seeds and dries the soil.

These are light times
    Times that make us blink and refocus
    That open up our vision, that show us the young sprouts we
        thought lost.

These are dark times. These are light times.

These are twisted, convoluted, divisive, intertwined,
    germinating, opening, flickering shadow and sunlight times.

Ongoing Reflection Questions, Suggestions, and/or Things to Think About

- These words are not about times of struggle between the light and the dark, with one being good and the other evil, but rather the struggle between evil – despair – apathy; and courage – joy – healing. Both are found in "light" and "dark." And the goodness found both in light and in dark is a dance with ribbons of light and dark that shelters, frees, that opens and embraces. I just simply got fed up with "dark" being equated with bad, and "light" with good. It just isn't so. What do you think?

- How might you describe the times we're living in?

- In the Christian tradition, at least, the image of "darkness" and "blackness" has been equated with evil, and bright light with goodness. How do you buck that tradition? In ancient times, the dark was a frightening time – no electric lights; when night closed in, it got really dim. And scary. But not so in our current times, in the space that many of us inhabit. Most of us can flip a switch and be comforted. So, how can we work with new images to create the same feeling? What are other words you could use to describe that feeling of helplessness, fear, shame, clouded vision, that the ancients meant when they said "dark"?

- For those of you in churches, or those of you engaging regularly in ritual, what are the symbols you could change over from the black/white dichotomy? In my church, we collected purple cloth to use in our sanctuary on Good Friday. In the past, we draped the church in black, but we've moving away from that. The symbols we show in our congregations matter.

- Based on this reading and your own reflections, do any scripture passages come to mind? These can be scriptures from a variety of religious traditions

Cutting Board

Something good is on my cutting board:
  Dried apricots, plump, sweet, into the oatmeal
  Carrots, crisp and precisely diced, into the lentil soup
  Pueblo green chili. Mmmm. This goes nearly anywhere!

Something necessary is on my cutting board:
  Healthy
  Warm.
  Spice and flavor.
  Homemade offering of time, stirring love.
  I cut up to create

Something decadent is on my cutting board:
Small squares of sweet chocolate mint fudge, to go into the
            freezer, to give away
  But first, a sample….or two…
  I cut up to break out of the ordinary.
  I cut up to give. To others. To myself.

Something that needs paring is on my cutting board:
  The butternut squash, to be cut into chunks and roasted for
            Thanksgiving dinner.
  But first, the rind to be pared off, peeling away the unnecessary,
      the bitter,
      that which would get in the way of flavor and warmth

Something occasionally true is on my cutting board:
  Something good and whole, yet needs cutting.
  Something best taken in, by hungry souls, only through cutting,
      paring away.
Is wholeness not all it's cracked up to be?
And small broken pieces of goodness what ultimately will feed us?

Ongoing Reflection Questions, Suggestions, and/or Things to Think About

- There's not necessarily any theological sophistication here; I was just looking for wisdom in the everyday acts of preparing various items of food for myself and others. Doing these everyday things can be just simply a time of reflection, a pause, maybe even a prayer.

- Where are the everyday moments that give you wisdom or that become occasions of prayer? And when are we all just overthinking things? ☺

- Based on this reading and your own reflections, do any scripture passages come to mind? These can be scriptures from a variety of religious traditions.

Crows

The crows in the tree swooped, and flapped and cawed harshly at me as I walked by, their displeasure quite evident. Ducking my head, I quickly crossed the street, away from their tree. They went silent and settled back down.

Apparently, I had ventured into their territory.

Apparently, they were nesting, and simply protecting their offspring.

In this, my urban neighborhood, the crows called out their ancient yet fresh instinct to protect their young. They would take on – very effectively – a creature many times their size to protect their young and their future (a sharp beak evens the odds a bit).

Sometimes it's not always easy to defend what we love. Sometimes, though, we do just that, unthinking and immediate. By instinct. Like the out flung arm of the parent protecting their child in the front seat, as the car comes to a sudden stop.

This is our nature: to protect what we love.

Can it also be our nature to extend what we love?

Beyond our own, also to those known and unknown, the familiar and the strange? The two-legged, four-legged, winged and finned, those that crawl upon the ground and swim in the seas?

Will we love these? Will we protect? What are we willing to risk to protect the future?

What will we do? What will we give to protect what we love? And how are we changed in the loving?

Ongoing Reflection Questions, Suggestions, and/or Things to Think About

- Think about the questions posed above. Write, draw, meditate, or in some other way, react to them, consider them, ponder them.

- Beyond your own immediate relationships, what/who do you love? Air, water, rattlesnakes, orangutans, mountains, trans youth, refugees? If you haven't already, do some research about those you love. Hold them in your heart, envision them safe and well. Think about how you might help make them so.

- Based on this reading and your own reflections, do any scripture passages come to mind? These can be scriptures from a variety of religious traditions.

Holy Distraction, Batman!

My morning devotional reading was interrupted
   – repeatedly –
by the distraction of the sunrise.

How do I attend to my prayers,
   to the theology of the written word,
   when the pinks and blues and golds
   persistently flow into me?

Oh. Right.

Ongoing Reflection Questions, Suggestions, and/or Things to Think About

- What ironic occurrences have pulled you up short into an "Oh, right" moment?

- Are you able to laugh at yourself, to not take yourself too seriously? That's really hard sometimes. What's your experience with that?

- What is holy, anyway? As you go through your day, try to see where the holy might be breaking in, where there might be sacred space, where embodiments of holy love might be seen. And, occasionally look in the mirror, and say, "Yes! Even here!"

- Based on this reading and your own reflections, do any scripture passages come to mind? These can be scriptures from a variety of religious traditions.

Oratorio

Coyote-song thrills back and forth across the road on cloudless
      summer dusk.
Broadly-banded layers of rose and orange, indifferent to our awe,
      fade over the mountains across the valley.

And, another song in another place:
Deceptive warmth on our shoulders, we hike the rock-steep path
      to the top.
Darkness falls, soft around the edges.
Then hundreds of thousands of bats pour out of the cave, their
      wing-song filling the entire sky.
      Voiceless, we shiver and witness.
      And in the dark, we make our way back down, songs
          ringing in our ears.

River-song curves the bottom of the canyon.
Tear swept vision of depth and beauty.
Indifferent to our awe, it blesses with rushing music.
In the shallows I fill my hat, anointing my head
Breathing again.

Drum-song in the adobe church Christmas Eve at the pueblo.
Unseen, it echoes off the walls.
As shivering witness, outsider and colonizer, I stand immobilized.
Heartbeat to heartbeat touches holiness and confession.

Song of sheer physicality, freedom, strength, and power,
    the humpback breaches, leaps from the chill Alaska waters.
Eight times for the sheer joy of the dance.
Miracle parting of the waters in leaps and turns, she graces us with
her presence,
    and then is gone, back to her calf,
to sing.

Ongoing Reflection Questions, Suggestions, and/or Things to Think About

- What are the different songs in your life? Are they songs of awe, confession, joy, confusion, questions, affirmation?

- As you move through your day, what songs might you hear? The radio or a playlist? The birds? The sound of traffic? How do they touch you?

- Do you think you might be a song for another?

- If you don't think you are musical, or don't really care for songs, what sounds or images might embrace you, might give you pause or make you think?

- Based on this reading and your own reflections, do any scripture passages come to mind? These can be scriptures from a variety of religious traditions.

O Beautiful and Wounded Creation:
A Prayer of Confession

*This was originally written as a group prayer. You can change the "we" to "I",
or you can read it as is, because it is all of us needing to pray this prayer.*

O beautiful and wounded Creation, we confess we have sinned
against you in thought, word, and deed, and in what we have done
and left undone.

We have imagined ourselves a species apart. We forget or deny that
we are all connected. We push away from each other out of fear or
greed or ignorance.

O beautiful and wounded Creation, you are Christ hanging on the
cross of wildfire-burned lands, parched with the thirst of drought,
life's blood draining away with the riverbeds gone dry, and dying
with each species gone extinct.

Your cry, O Christ, is the silence of extinction, the weeping of
dispossessed peoples.

O beautiful and wounded Creation:
> You land, water, air, seas;
> You who are torn by war, racism, deforestation, power,
> > disease
> You souls who cry out in hopelessness and fear, and you
> who have no voice,

We have sinned against you by what we have done and what we
have left undone.

We confess, dear God! We confess.

Turn us around, dear God, for it is not too late to mend and tend
your beautiful and wounded Creation.

Ongoing Reflection Questions, Suggestions, and/or Things to Think About

- Lament and confession are important – we are none of us perfect and we really screw things up sometimes, as individuals and as a species. But we can move on from lament to work for change, in ourselves and/or in our world. Don't get stuck in lament only, yet don't move too quickly to doing something, anything. It's a balance. It's a "both/and" situation. Grieve and work. Lament and act. And this prayer is written for a community – remember you are not alone.

- Based on this reading and your own reflections, do any scripture passages come to mind? These can be scriptures from a variety of religious traditions.

Angel Unaware

*Joyful, joyful, joyful
as only dogs know how to
be happy
With only the autonomy
of their shameless spirit
-- Pablo Neruda*

Nothing says "joyful" like a happy Labrador.
Spryly trotting down the path with your humans,
   big ole smile across your face,
      big ole tongue lolling out.
What glee!
   Barely containing your laughter, your delight.

You are so full of life.
It radiates out from you,
   glistens in your fur and in your deep, brown, soul-touching eyes.
Such joy!

Wide open to the world,
   your love overflows.

In the midst of turmoil and tension,
In the midst of fear and "othering":
   You pour your laughing heart out to anyone who will receive.

It is said you sense our feelings – you sense our pain and sorrow
         and fear
   So you curl your warm bodies next to us, growling at the
         shadows in the corner
Such love!

And you are wide open to the world,
   and your love overflows.

You dare, still, to keep smiling.

Ongoing Reflection Questions, Suggestions, and/or Things to Think About

- You may have noticed that I love dogs. You may feel the same way about dogs, too. Or cats, or gerbils, or parakeets, or snakes, or other critters.

- Write a love letter/thank you note to that being who pours (or poured) out its love to you, who touches/touched you with its laughing heart. Who helps/helped you keep smiling.

- Based on this reading and your own reflections, do any scripture passages come to mind? These can be scriptures from a variety of religious traditions.

Reflections on Mary Oliver's *Wild Geese*

(Google "Mary Oliver Wild Geese" to read the poem)

I thought of the poet Mary Oliver as I stood on the bridge looking down, down, at the Rio Grande Gorge, just outside of Taos, New Mexico. That grand river flowed on, oblivious to my existence or power. And I thought of Mary Oliver again as I stood at the bottom of the Grand Canyon and saw the Colorado River rushing past me, wonderfully ignoring my presence. In both cases, there appeared to me a magnificent and comforting indifference. "Meh. Not impressed. I'll just be flowing on past you thankyouverymuch."

I know we humans have an overpowering impact on river life, yet I was still struck with the indifference of this being – the river – and its own power. And in this indifference I heard, "You are part of us, if you would allow yourself to be, if you would step back from this mammoth (monstrous?) taking, and meld into the give and take. Welcome to the family of life. To the web of life. We will flow on past you, but you are part of us."

That is what, for me, is announcing my place "in the family of things" (Mary Oliver). I am simply part of it all, no more – and no less.

This brought me comfort, and a sense of rightness. And I couldn't put words to it until a friend opened my eyes to this fitting and holy bit of indifference.

It takes a community, another one, to open our eyes, and to touch our hearts. A community of two-legged, of 4-legged, even of 8-legged! A community of people, yes, but also a community of air and starlight, deep depths of the sacred darkness of space, and the hidden corners of the ocean. And rivers.

We are part of this web of life. Thanks be to God!

Ongoing Reflection Questions, Suggestions, and/or Things to Think About

- What is your community? Who has opened your eyes?

- Go stand by a river. Or, if that is not possible, the mighty Google can help you find river videos. Listen to the sounds of the river. Let yourself be mesmerized by the flowing of the water over rocks and into eddies. Don't let the mooning kayakers distract you (for long). Perhaps, silently, converse with the river. Or write down your thoughts. Or whip out your cellphone and take some pictures, playing with light and shadows. Somehow, interact (safely) with the river, for this is part of who you are.

- Based on this reading and your own reflections, do any scripture passages come to mind? These can be scriptures from a variety of religious traditions – even other poems by Mary Oliver!

The Cliff

(Hiking in Capitol Reef, Utah)

Who knew!
Hot dry sand in the bed of the wash, no rain, no flash flood

Cliff rose high
No noise, just rock and sand

Who knew?

Cliff rose high
Quiet rock by the side of the wash.

My hands touch one part, one piece of the warm rock.
Then,
    as one who waits,
    and waits a long time,
        but now joins with those hands
            (which touch one part, one piece, of warm rock),
      there is a rush of time, a thing from way, way back, a huge
             sense,
      a rush of time runs in my hands, my arms, my soul.

It's old. And wise. And She.
A crone of rock and ages.
      I could curl up in her lap, feel her arms hug my small self.
      Wise love and age and warm smile
      A "yes",
      A touch of warm rock, to one piece, one part of my soul

Ongoing Reflection Questions, Suggestions, and/or Things to Think About

- This actually happened – I touched the warm rock and this rush of awareness or something just streamed into me. I'm not usually given to mystical experiences, but this was powerful for me. Have you had any experiences like this? Doesn't need to have been "in nature"; it could be in a library doing research, or in a dream, or in a conversation.

- This ancient wisdom that I experienced was definitely feminine. What do you think about that? How does that make you feel? Is there a place in your spirituality for the divine feminine? Or for the divine non-binary, gender fluid?

- Based on this reading and your own reflections, do any scripture passages come to mind? These can be scriptures from a variety of religious traditions.

O Holy Snit

You can read and reflect over a period of three days *(Or read the whole thing in one sitting if you want to. That is how it was originally written.)*

Day One

The old story from the Christian Gospels tells of Jesus in Jerusalem during what we call "Holy Week": he enters the temple, and is enraged as he watches the money changers and those who sell the animals for sacrifice. He is enraged and chases them all out, and overturns their tables. He calls out their greed and dishonesty in one heck of a holy snit (well, actually, it was more than a snit). I imagine folks were talking about it for days to come, as they set their tables back up and went on with business as usual. Jesus called them out and threw them out, disrupting the system for a brief time.

Did it make any difference? Did anyone change? Who knows? But Jesus called them out because he knew you don't sit back from calling out injustice just because you think it won't make a difference.

Ongoing Reflection Questions, Suggestions, and/or Things to Think About

- Think about any activism events you may have been a part of – letter-writing, protests, civil disobedience, vigils – did they ever feel futile? Did you ever wonder if they made a difference? Did you do them anyway? Why? Or why not?

Day Two

There is a place in our faith and our transformational work for rage, for "calling b.s.", for calling out those who deceive, devalue, and devastate other people, creatures and eco-systems.

There is a place for rage — not violence, not hate, not self-righteousness — but rage.

And why not? Take a look at our nation's history around the use of fossil fuels. Industries and governments have known for decades that fossil fuels contribute hugely to climate change and its ensuing devastation. They *knew*. They lied. This has been well-documented.

Climate grief is real. So, too, is climate anger. So, yes, there is a place for outrage, for calling out lies, injustice, and devastation. There is a place for disruption and for upsetting the tables. There is a time to reject the status quo and Business as Usual.

There is a place for our rage that comes from deep grief, or from deep love. Or more likely, from both. Our rage comes from knowing it doesn't have to be this way, that innocents are being slaughtered through loss of habitat, pollution, and greed, and that there *can* be a better world, and we *can* be better people.

Ongoing Reflection Questions, Suggestions, and/or Things to Think About

- "Rage comes from knowing it doesn't have to be this way." Can you imagine a better way, a better world, a better people? To lighten this up a bit and come at it in a different way, pretend you're an alien from outer space (a Klingon, a Vulcan, or those cool blue Andorans with the antennae – you choose). And you come to visit Earth of the future because it's nearly a paradise, it's a good destination, a place you want to bring the kids. What makes it so? What does it look like? How is it different from now? In other words, try to imagine that better world, that better people.

Day Three

Sometimes our rage can be focused and channeled into constructive, fair, and just change – that is the goal. But sometimes our rage is so pain-filled that we need others to help us find safe spaces for it, and others who do the work of change for us for a time. Which brings us to community: "We are a gentle angry people, and we are singing for our lives," sings Holly Near. Amen! Yes. *We* sing *together*, as a people. We rage together as a people. We work together, as a people. For our lives. For Creation.

We're uncomfortable with rage. We want to move through it quickly and "get to the other side," to what we think is peace. "Why can't we be civil? Let's just come together." But at whose expense? What accountability and repair are we leaving out when we seek to be all nice and polite, or to stop dealing with uncomfortable situations?

There's a place in our work for rage. For discomfort. For a good, holy snit. We're in good company.

Ongoing Reflection Questions, Suggestions, and/or Things to Think About

- Today might be a good day to just move. Go outside and move through your neighborhood. Or stay at home and dance. Or do that aerobic exercise video you've been putting off. All this talk of anger and rage might get you squirmy or jumpy or antsy. (Or not.) And as you move, think about the communities you are a part of, that help you do your work in the world, and on yourself. Offer gratitude for the people that help you engage in constructive action, and who help bring you hope.

Based on the entire reading, and your own reflections, do any scripture passages come to mind? (Other than the Cleansing of the Temple one, of course!) These can be scriptures from a variety of religious traditions.

References providing some background for this essay:
"They Knew: The US Federal Government's Fifty-Year Role in Causing the Climate Crisis", James Gustave Speth, 2021.

"Singing for our Lives", Holly Near, 1978.

"Revolutionary Love", Valarie Kaur
https://valariekaur.com/revolutionary-love-project/

Two Domes

I took this photo one spring day in Washington DC, as I stepped outside of Union Station for a quick walk before boarding my train to continue a journey to see friends.

The parallels between the two domes struck me. Both these domes have been sources of conflict, of demonizing, of despair. One has power over the other; one pulls at our heartstrings perhaps more than does the other. One we would like to remove to a better life of peace and safety; one was nearly removed by a violent mob. Both contain human beings, flawed and gifted, hurting and strong, and all beloved by God.

Ongoing Reflection Questions, Suggestions, and/or Things to Think About

- What would you say to the people inside both those domes? What do you think they need to hear? What do you need to hear from them?

- If you haven't already, check out ways to get involved in the causes these domes represent – politics, democracy, voting, homelessness, food insecurity. If you're already doing some of this – well done! Celebrate that, and keep up the good work!

- Based on this reading and your own reflections, do any scripture passages come to mind? These can be scriptures from a variety of religious traditions.

Letting go and Taking in

Ponder these questions over a period of a few days.

We are always letting go and taking in. And we are always struggling with all the separations in our lives, all those issues or events that fracture our souls and our well-being. Politics comes to mind. As do "culture wars", addictions, fears, prejudices, resentments, faulty assumptions.

What do you need to let go of? What do you need to take in?

The "letting go":
- What is separating you from yourself?
- What is separating you from others?
- What is separating you from all Creation?

The "taking in":
- What can you try to do to bridge those separations?
- What do you need to help you do this?
- And what of beauty and life will you still celebrate and give thanks for, especially during these times?

Ongoing Reflection Questions, Suggestions, and/or Things to Think About

- Pray, meditate, listen to music, dance, as you think about these questions. Or sit quietly, light a candle, and think. Or talk with a friend about the questions.

- Make a collage of your responses, by drawing pictures, or cutting pictures from magazines that express your thoughts and feelings.

- Based on this reading and your own reflections, do any scripture passages come to mind? These can be scriptures from a variety of religious traditions.

Sacrament

Day One

<u>Here is what is:</u>
A sacrament is an "outward and visible symbol of an inner and spiritual grace." [*So say my seminary notes from over 40 years ago. See, it pays to save everything!*]

A sacrament is an outward sign of something holy going on inside.

That's nice.   No, really, it is.

An outward sign of the
  Holy churning away in you,
  Doing their good work.

In you. Yes, you.

You are a sacrament.

<u>Here is who you might be:</u>
All that is holy resides in you, as in all Creation.

(And as one who has struggled with low self-esteem all her life, I do like those words and I'm trying to believe them.)

(This is just to say that if you are questioning these words yourself, I get it.)

You are a sacrament.

A living, moving, loving, breathing, excreting sacrament.
(Alright, that was a bit gross but holy s#t! it's true).

You are
  all of you
  every little bit of you
A sacrament of choice:
  You can choose to say yes to the Holy within you.
  You can choose to be accomplice with the Holy working within you
  You can choose to be sacramental in your living;

69

in your ordinary, lovely, grimy, imperfect living.
  You are a sacrament

Immersed in the baptismal waters of your own gestation and birth, brought forth into life, and in your living, the salt tears of your own grief, wonder, joy and awe connect you to that ocean where all life began, and to all life itself.
(*Alright, that was a bit wordy*)

You are a sacrament.

Day Two

<u>Here's what you might do:</u>
Broken open by injustice or greed or fear or loss or by choice
  Poured out
    Self-giving
    Sometimes powerless
    Risking emptiness, and seeking to be filled again, by others.
    Feeding: others, yourself

  Through what you try to do in love and justice,
    you try to quench the hunger and thirst of those being drained
    by oppressive "isms",
    and by hate, exclusion and injustice that strikes like deadly
    bacteria.
  Challenging the ravenous hunger of greed and Business as Usual,
    refusing to feed *that* emptiness, but looking for the deeper need
    that might be tended.

You. Are. A. Sacrament.

What will you choose to do with that?

Ongoing Reflection Questions, Suggestions, and/or Things to Think About

- You are precious and powerful. Just sit with that for a bit.

- And because you are uniquely precious and powerful, you are called out to do something with that, for the sake of God's good Creation. Where do your great gifts meet the world's great need? (to paraphrase Frederick Buechner)

- Based on this reading and your own reflections, do any scripture passages come to mind? These can be scriptures from a variety of religious traditions.

Just Stop.

Just stop.

Put this down. Go outside and move around as you are able.
If you're still in your PJs, you may want to get dressed first.
If there's a blizzard out there or a torrential downpour, or it's already
over 95° out, stop anyway. Look out the window. Move around.

Just stop.

Breathe.

Empty your mind. Just feel.

Come back to readings and questions tomorrow.

Just be.

Thoughts on Pouring a Cup of Coffee

Rich earthen deep brown
Warmth cascading, embracing
Like a sacrament…

…Or an afterthought?
Unthinking, unmindfully
What am I missing?

What does it matter?
What is pouring out, spilling?
Lifeblood of others?

Rainforest life, worth.
Draining dreams, existence?
Choices do matter.

Rich earthen deep brown
Lives intertwined, my power
To empower others

In this small sip, I will try.
No, I will work, act.
Not an afterthought.

Make of this a sacrament
And a deep promise.

Ongoing Reflection Questions, Suggestions, and/or Things to Think About

- Look into whether or not your coffee is Fair Trade. According to the Grounds for Change website (https://groundsforchange.com), the certification of "fair trade" lets you know the origin of a product. It has certain standards centered on workers' rights, sustainable practices, and fair prices for the coffee growers.

- Fair Trade coffee is often more expensive than conventional coffee. So, is this a justice issue for those people and businesses who buy coffee in your community? The solution is not to stop buying Fair Trade, but to make it possible for more people/businesses to purchase Fair Trade coffee. How might that happen in your community?

- Now, put your feet up, and have a cup of coffee. It's ok. Enjoy it. Think about these issues, take action as you can, and give thanks for this marvelous brew and those who make it possible. But don't do this too late in the day, or you'll never get to sleep tonight!

- Based on this reading and your own reflections, do any scripture passages come to mind? These can be scriptures from a variety of religious traditions.

Habitat Loss

As forests are clear cut, there's habitat loss.

As more and more homes are built in more and more wilderness places, there's habitat loss.

As coral reefs bleach, rivers dry up, pollutants poison wetlands, there's habitat loss.

As earthquakes shatter cities and towns, there's habitat loss.

As war uproots families and entire communities, there's habitat loss.

As rising sea levels, hurricanes, and massive flooding drive people from their homes, there's habitat loss.

Habitat loss – it isn't just for critters anymore.

We, too, are creatures of Earth, and we're losing our habitat. We are all connected. Even in the wrenching loss of our own habitat, we are connected to the greater web of life.

Ongoing Reflection Questions, Suggestions, and/or Things to Think About

- Does it seem strange to think of humans as having "habitats" like animals do? And to experience habitat loss? Humans are losing their habitats at an alarming rate through war, famine, desertification, violence, flooding, and rising sea levels.

- We are all in this together, in grief and loss. Think (or feel) about it. Perhaps saving one habitat will save the other.

- In a lighter vein, but still profound, there's The Wombat. Take a look at the video: https://vimeo.com/54435965 (Sometimes the link doesn't work; it's an old video, so just Google The Wombat All Is One). It's a short video, about a minute long, talking about connectedness. In a couple hundred words, it pretty much says it all.

- Based on this reading and your own reflections, do any scripture passages come to mind? These can be scriptures from a variety of religious traditions.

Prayer

How do moose pray?

Do they even need to?
Are they so in touch with the Creator, that no words are needed,
   like an old couple who have seen it all, been through it all,
   connected to each other down to their cells,
yet always surprised by something new?
Like that.

How do moose pray? Or dogs? Or sand on the beach?
        Or pollinators, or winter,
        or music, flowers, dirt,
        our hearts?

Is all of life a prayer bowl, resonating, wordlessly, eternally?
The sound ripples in an ever-widening circle,
   like the candle flame's halo –
        holy, warm, never really disappearing.

Ongoing Reflection Questions, Suggestions, and/or Things to Think About

- Carry on a conversation with the moose (or the pollinators, or the dirt, etc.) about their prayer life.

- What does prayer mean to you? How do you pray? Do you pray? Would you like to?

- What about prayer makes you anxious, upset or angry? What about prayer gives you life?

- Based on this reading and your own reflections, do any scripture passages come to mind? These can be scriptures from a variety of religious traditions.

Blessing of our Animal Companions

Excerpted and adapted from Blessing of the Animals: A Celebration in Two Parts,
https://allyson.revsawtell.org/blessing-of-the-animals-a-celebration-in-two-parts/

Day One

I parakeet-sat for friends once, a long time ago, shortly after our beloved dog died. Each morning, I'd let Budgie out of his cage. He would stand on the table while I read the morning newspaper. Sometimes he'd try to nibble on my cereal. Occasionally he did more than just stand on the newspaper. But we co-existed well, and I missed him when his family came home. That small creature was an enormous presence, comfort, and joy. An enormous blessing.

I've had dogs throughout my life. A bird or two. A rabbit. And a turtle that disappeared one day and was never seen again. All animal companions, and in ways great and small, they were enormous blessings. The prayer below is for them, and for your animal companions, or your friends' animal companions, or the animal companions you once had, or the ones that someday may enter your life. And for those domesticated animals we might not think are "our animal companions" but are with us as they sustain us in body and spirit.

A Prayer of Gratitude and Celebration
This was originally done as a congregational prayer, so you can read it like that, knowing you are in community with animal-lovers everywhere!

We are grateful, O holy one, for the animals in our lives! The birds that sing to us and sometimes talk back to us. The cat who may ignore us but loves us all the same, and cries when we leave.

We thank you, O holy one, for our animal companions. The fish who flash their bright colors in the bowl, who are pictures of grace and beauty (at least until they go belly up one day). The huge dogs who think they are lap dogs, the small ones who think they are giant guard dogs – and all in between, who grace us and love us beyond anything we deserve.

We offer prayers of gratitude for beloved service animals that keep us safe and stable, who walk with us when our steps falter, or our fear paralyzes. Who guide us, calm our fears, and let us know when someone's at the door.

We give thanks, O holy one, for our animal companions, those with us now, those gone before, and those yet to enter our lives.

Day Two

We give you thanks, O holy one, for those domesticated animals who give so much to us whether they want to or not. May we work to see that humane conditions prevail for them. We are thankful for their profound gifts.

For the bees and their honey, for chickens and their eggs, we give thanks. For cattle, pigs, poultry, and fish and all other animals who give their entire lives for our nourishment and well-being, we give bittersweet and humble thanks.

For silk worms and alpacas, we give thanks! For sheep and their wool, for goats and their milk (and their hilarious YouTube videos), we give thanks.

We are grateful and honor all their gifts and their sacrifices. Thank you, O holy one, for all the animals in our lives! In humility and gratitude, we offer this prayer. Amen!

Ongoing Reflection Questions, Suggestions, and/or Things to Think About

- If you have a favorite picture of a pet or a friend's pet, or some such item, put it where you can see it as you read through this. If you have a pet nearby that will let you pat them and "love them up" as you read this, do so (you may need to bribe them with treats...).

- Talk to your pet. Sing to them, if you wish (my beloved mother-in-law used to sing to her dogs and I learned from her that it was OK to do that.)

- Recently Colorado passed a law that required Colorado farm owners or operators to abide by specific conditions like spacing egg-laying hens at least one foot apart from each other, and to raise only cage-free hens. Or to buy from only cage-free, humanely raised producers. What other sorts of legislation have you heard of that seeks to create more humane conditions for domesticated animals?

- It's a bittersweet, hard balance between creating humane conditions, and then killing the critters for our dinner tables. I do eat meat, and I think about this a lot. When I've been called on to pray over a church dinner I have usually included something like, "And we thank you for the creatures and gifts of the field who gave their lives to nourish us." This may be a bit of a buzz-kill for a Thanksgiving feast, but it's important to remember.

- Based on this reading and your own reflections, do any scripture passages come to mind? These can be scriptures from a variety of religious traditions.

Step Out of Yourself

Step out of yourself.
Leave your skin behind
 (oh, and all the rest, the messy bits)
Be pure spirit.

That doesn't work for most of us, does it?
We are of earth, after all, of matter. Embodied.

Even as we are also of stardust and spirit, we are rooted in matter.

And matter is built on the interplay of relationships, molecule by
        molecule.

Still, step outside of *yourself.*
  Your solitary self.
  Your *one* being.
See who you truly are:
  Rooted in stardust, dirt, rocks, grasses, forests – connected to
        them all.
Connected to each other.

Claim who you truly are:
  Not just a unique and glorious "I", but part and parcel of "we"
        and "us."

Ongoing Reflection Questions, Suggestions, and/or Things to Think About

- Tonight, look outside your window and see if you can see some stars or planets (this may be hard, but even in urban areas you might see a few). Listen to the wind, or the calm, or the noisy neighbors. But focus mainly on the stars and darkness. Imagine them reaching out to you in a caress, an embrace. Send your heart's love out into that vast emptiness, for there is nowhere that God isn't. And you are connected to the stars and the night, and even the noisy neighbor.

- Based on this reading and your own reflections, do any scripture passages come to mind? These can be scriptures from a variety of religious traditions.

Prayer of Confession and Lament

How does confession embrace all of creation?
Words are so small
Ice so thin it will not move
Tears melting unshed

We want to avoid this pain if at all possible but it needs to soak
        into the parched earth,
            into the thin layers of cold and despair because it cannot
                be turned away.

Like a glacier slowly advancing, the future crawls out in front of us
        but wait,
           the glacier is retreating, the future is shrinking
                we're skating on thin ice.

We want to avoid this pain if at all possible but it needs to soak into
        the parched earth, into the thin layers of cold and despair
        because it will not be turned away.

Oh God of snow and ice, of rain and ocean, of tears and barren
        ground, we face the rising oceans
and the melting ice with fear, grief, anger, helplessness. We seek the
        comfort of denial and
Business as Usual, and we know that is not the answer.

So we confess.

We confess that the workings of our institutions and systems, the
use of our own power, the choices we make, the actions we take –
or do not take – contribute to the devastation of all you love.

O God of hope and healing, words are not enough. Thoughts and
prayers are not enough.

We need to change as a country, as a species, and that terrifies us
        because we do not know what
that looks like or how to do it.

So we watch the glaciers disappear, and feel sad or scared or
powerless.

And the future waits for us and seems to shrink.

And with each flawed system, each misuse of power, each choice,
    each action or inaction that
gives us a way out, a sense of comfort, a denial of the desperate
    urgency, the future waits for us.

And we try not to hear its cries.

Ongoing Reflection Questions, Suggestions, and/or Things to Think About

- Call someone up, or email them. Go out for coffee (or ice cream). Talk about this with someone you trust and love and respect. You may simply say, "Wow, this is a real bummer of a prayer!" and just go ahead and scarf down your double-scoop mint-chocolate chip ice cream *[I may have been projecting a bit just then...]* Or you may delve deeper into the conversation.

- Based on this reading and your own reflections, do any scripture passages come to mind? These can be scriptures from a variety of religious traditions.

Wolves

We were at the zoo at dusk, visiting the wolf enclosure, with its trees and large rocks, and forest floor. Along with families and small children, we watched in awe as these gorgeous creatures sat, slept, basically ignored us, and occasionally trotted on by.

Then, one wolf emerged from the trees, with a freshly-killed rabbit in its jaws. Families and small children squealed in horror and disgust.

"Ah," I thought, "The cycle of life."

Unwary rabbit and apex predator; we're all in this together (some, apparently, for a shorter span of time).

Ongoing Reflection Questions, Suggestions, and/or Things to Think About

- Admit it. You love watching those nature films with the lioness chasing down the gazelle, right? Or the spider trapping the unwary fly (that might be a little easier to watch than the poor gazelle). Or maybe not. Maybe you want to run right up and chase the lioness away. But chasing the lioness away means the predator and her family run the risk of starving, while the gazelle population runs the risk of growing to an unsustainable size and they starve, too. The cycle of life can sometimes suck, if you're the gazelle or the fly. But it maintains the balance. The balanced dance of predator and prey, although gruesome and sad, allows life to flourish.

- For example, killing off prairie dogs (which goes on all the time), runs the risk of causing collapse of an area's eco-system. Prairie dogs are a "keystone species", species that other animals and plants depend on to survive. Hawks, coyotes, foxes, worms, plants all depend on prairie dogs. Over 150 species of plants and animals are associated with prairie dog colonies, and when prairie dogs die off, those 150 species in that area are threatened. And prairie dogs are just one, cute, furry, small species. There are many, many other examples of connectedness within the web of life. Google "wolf elk songbirds Yellowstone" or "grizzly bears salmon riparian zones" to learn about other such connectedness in Creation.

- Based on this reading and your own reflections, do any scripture passages come to mind? These can be scriptures from a variety of religious traditions.

Sacred Song and Holy Ground

Sacred place, holy song – I need you to live.

Coyote-song,
River-song.
Whale-song.
Wing-song.
Drum-song.

Heartbeat.

We suspect there are so many things we have yet to learn.
A vital part we have yet to learn.

Sacred song and holy ground – I need you to live.

Mountains have layers of meaning;
    Strong, deep history grounded in place graces us with her
        presence.
Blesses.

We shiver and witness.

So many things indifferent to our awe.
  Songs ringing,
  Tear-swept vision soft around the edges.

Shiver and witness.

I need you to live.

Ongoing Reflection Questions, Suggestions, and/or Things to Think About

- This reading is a "Collage Poem." It was a "poetry prompt" I found on a poetry-prompt website, and it's credited to First Nations poet Liz Howard. The prompt instructs you to take one page each from a journal, a science-fiction novel, and one of your own poems. Then you pull out words and phrases that jump out at you, and write a poem using them. For this reading, I used a page from Archeology Southwest Magazine, "The Fifth Season" by N.K. Jemisin, and my poem "Oratorio" (which is elsewhere in this devotional guide). If you like to write, try this prompt sometime.

- "I need you to live" can be read two ways – in order to live, I need you (you = sacred song and holy place). Or, I need *for* you to live. When I checked the work from which this line came, it was ambiguous, too, as well.

- What do you need to live?

- What is a sacred space for you? What is, for you, a holy song?

- Based on this reading and your own reflections, do any scripture passages come to mind? These can be scriptures from a variety of religious traditions.

What Shall We Celebrate Today?

Each day, at the bottom of my computer screen, there is a graphic that appears in the "Type here to search" bar, courtesy of the Mighty Microsoft. You probably have one, too!

If you hover over said graphic, an interesting factoid appears, accompanied by a photograph and related links. Things like "World Tiger Day", or "National Roller Coaster Day." Sometimes it's about a city in India or Montana. Sometimes it's something about oceans, or mountains. This is really kind of cool.

I've taken to checking this out every morning as I settle in to read our online Denver Post. And as I click on the graphic, I find myself saying, "And what are we celebrating today, hmm?" I like that feeling. I like that question. What are we celebrating? What is being called to my attention that I might have missed?

It's a helpful reminder as I read through the morning paper and immerse myself in the angst of our beloved planet and all its creatures, human and other than human.

What are we celebrating today? A moment of grace. Of gratitude. And maybe some new information.

Who knew that something so secular from the Mighty Microsoft could be a vehicle for grace?

Ongoing Reflection Questions, Suggestions, and/or Things to Think About

- What unexpected spaces or events have touched you in ways that call forth gratitude?

- What do you want to celebrate right now? What to you *need* to celebrate right now? Is it even too difficult to think of celebrating?

- Does celebration feel like a denial of Creation's pain, your pain, others' pain? It does not need to be a denial, but instead a way of affirming life and hope, and a commitment to do the work that's needed to tend to and alleviate the world's pain.

- What are you grateful for now, in this moment? Look around you. What is one thing, no matter how small, that you are grateful for?

- Based on this reading and your own reflections, do any scripture passages come to mind? These can be scriptures from a variety of religious traditions.

Prayer of Thanksgiving for the Wild Creatures

Excerpted and adapted from Blessing of the Animals: A Celebration in Two Parts, https://allyson.revsawtell.org/blessing-of-the-animals-a-celebration-in-two-parts/

I give thanks for the wild creatures:
  The whale, wolf, wolverine, wombat
  The tiger, tarantula, tapir and termite
  The aardvark, alligator, alpaca and anaconda,
  The majestic, graceful, powerful and strong ones,
  The small, quick, nimble and nearly-unseen ones,
  The gross, slippery, squirmy and slimy ones

I give thanks for the wild creatures:
  The scary and the scared – all sacred
  The predator and prey – all precious
  The lovely and the funny-looking – all beautiful.

Oh God, the miracles of creation, evolution, instinct, and life are all around us.

With grateful heart, I celebrate.

I give thanks for the wild creatures! Amen!

Ongoing Reflection Questions, Suggestions, and/or Things to Think About

- Sometime today, try to read up on some wild creature you don't know much about. The Snail Darter, the Greater Prairie Chicken, the Sea Cucumber come to mind for me.

- Think of animals that really terrify you: spiders, snakes, leeches, big dogs, wasps…whatever really scares you. Work on offering a prayer of gratitude for their place in the web of life, even if you don't exactly know what that place is (maybe do some research). They, too, are beloved children of God (I have tried this with certain politicians, too, with some limited success. The animals are easier.)

- Based on this reading and your own reflections, do any scripture passages come to mind? These can be scriptures from a variety of religious traditions.

During a stressful evening watching certain politicians and candidates on the evening news

How to listen without hate?
How to listen without rage?

I hear hate clothed in rationale and reason.
So polite. It's all "for the people."
Who the hell are the people?

"They" bring out the worst in me.
How do I rise above it?
How do I not sink to their level?

How do I listen when I am so filled with rage? I get triggered at the first words.

Then, I can't write.
How can you make poetry out of hate? Or liturgy from rage?

In my calmer moments, I know that my rage comes from a deeper place of pain, fear, helplessness, disempowerment. My rage is actually deep lament.

Huh. You *can* make poetry out of rage, liturgy from lament.

It's called a Psalm.

It's called a "My God, my God, why have you forsaken me?!" moment.

It actually feels like lament takes less energy than does hate.
But lament has more purpose than hate, more good to come from it, more strength and power.

Ongoing Reflection Questions, Suggestions, and/or Things to Think About

- I think these words ring true regardless of where you are on the political spectrum. Just thought I'd say that.

- I wrote this piece while I was indeed watching the evening news. It was an attempt, at first, to calm myself down. I was so filled with rage and hate I thought I'd explode. Then I made myself try to be vulnerable to the pain that was underneath my rage. So I hid away for a while, in my room, listened to myself, and wrote those words.

- What triggers you? Who is the "other" for you, the "they"?

- Try to write your own Psalm of lament – it could be personal, or about something societal or systemic. What is wrenching at your soul?

- If you're not into writing, use some other means of expression – music, dance, drawing, for example.

- Read one of the Psalms of lament in the Bible (like Psalm 22, or 42, or 43). Have a conversation with the person speaking those words. Play the part of that person's friend, or family member – or God.

- Or just, simply, breathe. Just breathe.

Sacred Heart

What breaks your heart? What holds your heart? What heals your
 heart?

Ancient Israelites had it right –
 the heart is not the seat of emotion, but of will.

Love at its best feels really good
 Caress of a lover
 Puppies crawling all over you
 Laughter with friends

But love is first and foremost an act of will – willing the good for
 another.
What, then, breaks your will? What holds your will?
What heals your will?
What touches your will and gives it power, strength?

Speak softly to your heart gentle words of fierce determination and
 affirmation and hope.

Hope *in* your heart, your will, your strength.
Hope *in* the hearts of others.
Hope *in* the heart of God – that indescribable force bending
 towards justice and connectedness.
 Join in, link up.

Don't be party to heartbreak.
 You will participate in grief, but do not participate in the
 breaking of another's will.

Sacred heart – holiness in what it *could* choose – connectedness and
 integrity: love.
 Even as tattered heart, wounded heart, but not isolated heart.

What breaks your heart?
What holds your heart?
What heals your heart?

Ongoing Reflection Questions, Suggestions, and/or Things to Think About

- Simply reflect on the questions in this reading. What jumps out at you? What do you want to respond to? What do you find unsettling and that you'd rather ignore?

- Take a couple days with this. Day One is for Lament. What breaks your heart? Something done to you? Seeing a loved one disintegrate before your eyes? Hearing of yet another species gone extinct, another fentanyl overdose, another indigenous woman gone missing, another trans youth attacked….The list of heartbreak goes on.

- By way of reflecting, perhaps cut out a heart shape, and write all that on it, all that breaks your heart. Rip it up; your heart is broken, after all. Lament and cry out! You are in the best of biblical tradition with this. And you may want to do this in solitude. At home. Not on the bus. Be safe as you do this.

- This day, for a time, live with the lament, and KNOW THAT LAMENT IS NOT THE END OF THE STORY. And, *if you live with ongoing severe depression*, be careful, maybe even skip this exercise. You've had enough lament already. Move towards the "what heals your heart" questions instead.

- The next day, sit with the beginnings of hope. Reflect on the questions: What heals your heart? How might you, yourself, be a healer for some person or creature? How might you be an instrument of peace? What might you hope *in*? Where do you find your strength?

- Is there a piece of music, a book, or a movie that soothes your soul, or that affirms the reality of goodness and love in the world? Listen/read/view that resource.

- Breathe. Stretch. Eventually recommit to entering into the healing work we're all called to do.

- Based on this reading and your own reflections, do any scripture passages come to mind? These can be scriptures from a variety of religious traditions.

Prayer for Community:
Lament and Affirmation

We are not alone! This is our cry. And this is our call.

We are not alone, and we owe each other life and love and hope and promise.

It is through us, together – all beings of flesh and blood and stone and water and air and bark and leaf – that life can flourish.

Together with that unknown mystery that surrounds all of life, this embrace of the Love that we call God, life can flourish.

We need each other.

We are, and have always been, beings of community. We are, and have always been, living within the web of all life. And we have forgotten that. Or denied it. Or ignored it.

As a species, we have thought so very deeply: "I am all that is. I am all that matters." In our own humano-centrism, we don't realize how isolated we have become from each other: we don't even recognize the web of life through which we move, so we rip the strands and fray the ties that hold us all together.

We've lost so much. And we don't even realize how much that hurts.

There is a depth of loneliness so profound that we do not acknowledge it except in waves of fear or dominance or power over.

We have forgotten. Or denied. Or ignored.

So we come together to remember and to re-member ourselves. We have to collect the frayed pieces of the web of life, and tenderly weave them together again and make a new creation. We have to soak the strands with our tears, softening the fibers so we can weave each other again.

We are connected to each other! This is our cry. And this is our call.

We are connected to each other, and we owe Creation life and love and hope and promise.

Ongoing Reflection Questions, Suggestions, and/or Things to Think About

- Remember those little red and green paper Christmas chains you may have made as a child? You get to do it again! Or for the first time. Cut up strips of paper (4-6 inches long). You can use scratch paper, construction paper, old church bulletins, or whatever you have lying around the house.

- On each one, write one thing that you are connected to or that helps you feel connected to others – a person, or a special place, an animal, a memory, a song, a community, an action. Do a different one for each scrap of paper.

- After you've written on each slip of paper, roll one of the slips into a circle, and tape it together. Put the next strip of paper through that circle, and tape that one to itself. Now you've got two interlocking circles of paper and the beginning of a chain. Add the next strip, and so on, and by now you hopefully have a chain. It doesn't have to be a long one.

- Hang that up somewhere, or put it on a corner of your desk or on your bookshelf. Every time you see it, breathe out gratitude for all those precious things and beings that connect you to something greater than yourself, that are pieces of love and community in your life. How can you add onto this chain and make it even longer? And, perhaps, come Christmas time, you can decorate your tree with this!

- You can also cut up more strips of paper, and on these you can write one thing that you feel separated from, alienated from, cut off from. As before, write a different one on each piece of paper, but this time, keep the strips as they are, and put them in a bowl or tape them up separately on the wall, or stick them in an envelope. Keep this next to your "connectedness" chain, and spend some time thinking about those things you've written down. Lament, or confess, and think about what you can do to help dismantle the "separation" pieces, to change those pieces. What would that take?

- Or simply, just sit with this reading. Close your eyes and see what images might appear as you reflect on the reading.

- Based on this reading and your own reflections, do any scripture passages come to mind? These can be scriptures from a variety of religious traditions.

The Bison and Other Vignettes
(Sights and Sounds at Tetons/Yellowstone National Parks)

The sound came first, deep-throated purr
And wild, not tame, or mine
My awe released towards this gorgeous beast
He gracefully grazed on his verdant feast
His presence there a shrine

Stirring of brush, and muted sound
Soft, rounded tones, an embrace
The grouse turned away with a gentle sway
Towards the forest, although I hoped she'd stay,
But left with me her grace

The moose stood by the pond, alone
Indifferent to us, I saw
And rightly so, for in her world, I know
I will never belong nor should I go
But stand in prayerful awe

Ongoing Reflection Questions, Suggestions, and/or Things to Think About

- In this poem, I tried to express the wonderful indifference of the animals to the people around them. I wanted to emphasize their own integrity, separate from the human race. We humans are simply part of the Web of Life, not the center, or the top, or the main attraction. For me, there is something comforting in that. We are part of the same community of Creation, all of us. Do you agree? How would you express this differently?

- I also know that we humans do have power over all of these creatures, even the Grizzly Bears I was lucky enough to NOT run into in Yellowstone, although I would have loved to see them. Any one of those creatures, no matter how huge, I could kill with a single gunshot (or someone could, I've never held a gun). Ultimately we do have power over them, whether it's in immediate physical violence, or the effects of habitat reduction and species extinction. How does that make you feel?

- Based on this reading and your own reflections, do any scripture passages come to mind? These can be scriptures from a variety of religious traditions.

Wholly Wonder

The Golden puppy didn't know what to make of her first snow fall.
　　So she jumped at the snowflakes, one by one,
　　　trying to grasp, to savor, to play.

Curiosity. Mystery.　Gotta explore.

What other response is there, really?

You don't ignore something as wondrous and mysterious
　　as this cold white stuff flowing all around you.

She snuffled and spun, scrutinizing and investigating,
　　filling her being with grace-filled new experience, joyfully
　　wrapped in mystery and curiosity.

When our son first discovered sunbeams, he cooed.

Rapt. Fascinated. Looking deeply.
　　(He did the same when he noticed for the first time that those
　　things flopping in front of him
　　belonged to *him*, looking with fascination at his fingers and
　　thumbs.)

Aren't these all holy responses to complete, entire, surprising
miracles?

How else to respond to the miracle of Creation all around us, but
to take it in, savor it,
　　hearts leaping in wonder,
　　and give voice to awe.

Ongoing Reflection Questions, Suggestions, and/or Things to Think About

- Oh, go ahead! Watch some baby goat videos, or puppy videos or cat videos. The ones where they explore and play. Or animals in the wild, playing or nuzzling (killing prey is for another time…). Monterey Bay Aquarium has some great jellyfish videos https://www.montereybayaquarium.org/animals/live-cams/moon-jelly-cam

- What, in the creaturely world brings you a sense of wonder? The critters are experiencing their own wonder apart from any of us, yet sometimes we get to witness it. What a gift!

- Now, how to take the step, to keep from viewing Nature as "surface", entertainment, or simply cute, but to realize that we are part of this web, this sacred space? We are connected, which means we are part of the wonder, as well.

- How do you respond to the miracle of Creation all around us and in us and through us?

- Based on this reading and your own reflections, do any scripture passages come to mind? These can be scriptures from a variety of religious traditions.

Blessing of the Wild Ones

Excerpted and adapted from Blessing of the Animals: A Celebration in Two Parts, https://allyson.revsawtell.org/blessing-of-the-animals-a-celebration-in-two-parts/

This is a time for a blessing of the animals. And this is the time, also, for the blessing OF the animals, for they are a blessing just by being. They are a blessing within the web of life, in that careful and miraculous dance of a balanced eco-system. Like God, they create order out of chaos, whether they are predator or prey. So celebrate the blessings that are the wild creatures of God's good Creation.

Take a moment to visualize some wild creatures, or to recall moments when you've been in closer contact with wild creatures than you normally are, or times when you've looked outside your window in the late evening and seen a fox or a raccoon. I even saw a couple of coyotes one early morning, in my Denver city neighborhood! Or simply the times you watched the birds at the birdfeeder. They are fascinating creatures. My in-laws once watched a bear at their birdfeeder. But I digress....

This is a time for a blessing of the wild ones in silence and distance:
...by silent witness to their presence
...by closing down speech and the need to be center, and just to listen, to look, to witness
Here is blessing.

The nature of the wild things is just to be – not to be just for us, but just to be.
And simply by being
  – irrespective of us
  – indifferent to us
  – wary, sometimes of us – or maybe curious
  – just simply by being
Here is blessing.

And we are blessed.

Ongoing Reflection Questions, Suggestions, and/or Things to Think About

- The nature of the wild things is to be in relationship, in give and take, predator and prey. The nature of wild things is to embody the web of life, knowing instinctively that one cannot survive alone. As apex predator, where do we humans fit in? How are we to live in relationship with all wild things?

- Gray wolves have been reintroduced in Colorado. This is not an easy issue. Wolves bring important balance to eco-systems, yet ranchers are affected when they lose a calf or a dog to a wolf. What does it mean to coexist with wild creatures? Are we humans encroaching on their territory?

- Based on this reading and your own reflections, do any scripture passages come to mind? These can be scriptures from a variety of religious traditions.

We Don't Have Time
for a Tame Church

Being the Church in this time of climate crisis

We don't have time for a tame church. Antiseptic. Avoiding things too hard to hear.

"The words are too hard. They will stop listening," I was told once by a pastor.

Maybe the problem is not with the message itself, but with those who won't hear the message. Maybe the problem is with the community that doesn't embody the kind of space where people are safe to hear, feel, and react to the message. Maybe we need to move on beyond those who won't hear, and engage those who will.

We don't have time for a tame church, with a message that falls lightly on the ears and pats the heart reassuringly.

We need a church that is nothing less than hands held out, holding each other up as the winds threaten to blow us off the edge. Nothing less than an embrace as our hearts are shredded and we wonder where – and how – and if – we go on from here.

Nothing less than a community with a story about life flourishing, and an identity founded in love.

A community that insists on hope.

Nothing less than imperfect courage.

Nothing less than a beloved community

Nothing less than a community that laughs anyway.

We don't have time for a tame church, earnest and inoffensive.

We need a church that is nothing less than a community living in the context of a torn world of loss and despair, a world that will never be the same – but a world so loved that we keep moving through it to envision and join in creating something new.

Living in that context but incongruously still believing there can be a new world – grieving the losses of species and homelands, and saying "No more!"

We don't have time for a tame church.

Ongoing Reflection Questions, Suggestions, and/or Things to Think About

- So, what's your reaction?

- If you are part of a faith community, what is your community saying (or not saying) about climate change, environmental devastation and injustice, climate grief, lament and hope?

- Based on this reading and your own reflections, do any scripture passages come to mind? These can be scriptures from a variety of religious traditions.

Dear Silence

To paraphrase sister Audre,
You're going to be afraid anyway,
   so you might as well speak.

Say goodbye to silence.

Dear silence,
   There are times when I rest in your arms, open to the universe that bends towards justice and is the ground and deep well of love.

Dear silence,
   There are times when only you can speak, and can speak only when I welcome you in.

Dear silence,
   Sometimes you have sheltered me, a child afraid, and your arms have protected me.
   And sometimes that's ok.

But sheltered in the confines of you, not to be seen or heard, never extending beyond my reach, you shout of disbelief in what is possible.

So when self-doubt demands my silence –
   Goodbye.

And when the personal becomes political and the silence in me silences, you do not protect or heal.

When privilege and fear demand my silence, you do not protect or heal.

When Business As Usual beckons with seductions of muted comfort and safety, you do not protect or heal.

Dear silence,
   Goodbye.

   I stand in your shadow and swallow my voice. And then it festers and twists.

Dear silence,
   Goodbye.

On my brave days, in my mind's eye, I take a breath, I shed the silence, I tremble and claim my voice.

Dear silence,

  Thank you for those moments you did no damage, but sheltered for a time. I'll call you when I need you.

  Until then, goodbye.

Ongoing Reflection Questions, Suggestions, and/or Things to Think About

- "Audre" as referenced above, is Audre Lorde. She was a self-described "black, lesbian, mother, warrior, poet." And she was, at one point, a librarian, which makes me love librarians all the more! Look her up. She was one of the prophets of our time. One of her more famous quotes is "My silences had not protected me. Your silence will not protect you." (From Audre Lorde, "The Cancer Journals"). That quote was what inspired today's reflection.

- When have you kept silence, yet wanted to speak or make some noise? When were you silenced by others? When have you silenced others?

- Make a pact with yourself to attempt two things this week: Muster the courage to speak up at an occasion when silence seems more comfortable. And, at another occasion, take a breath and close your mouth when you see that others need to be heard, too.

- Based on this reading and your own reflections, do any scripture passages come to mind? These can be scriptures from a variety of religious traditions.

Coyote Song

It started with one lone howl,
   Beyond the side of the path,
   During a brilliant, orange-rose dusk in late summer.

The coyote howled.

Then across the path, on the other side, came the unseen, lone response.

And then the whole chorus: yips, howls, barks. Glorious!

Marking territory, perhaps.
Or hunting.
Or simply to call to each other and gather their pack around them.

Something was heard, felt, expressed. Connections made.

Gradually the sounds died away. Night fell.
The hunt was over. The prey discovered?
Boundaries set?
Community assured?
Who knows.

They were doing their work.
And by sheer luck, we were there to witness their song.
It was a blessing.

Ongoing Reflection Questions, Suggestions, and/or Things to Think About

- What sounds bring to you a sense of awe and gratitude? Animal sounds? Certain music? The voice of a beloved? The falling of rain?

- These sounds don't need to be quiet and calming. I am partial, as you can see from the reading above, to the sounds of coyotes howling. And to bagpipes. I love bagpipe music. Sounds can be tranquil, stirring, harmonious or discordant. What touches your heart and makes you glad, and grateful?

- Write about these sounds. Or listen to them. Or draw them, if you are so inclined. Make a playlist, if you are able. How can these sounds be incorporated into your prayer/devotional life?

- Based on this reading and your own reflections, do any scripture passages come to mind? These can be scriptures from a variety of religious traditions.

Seasonal

As you find yourself approaching certain holiday seasons while moving through this devotional guide, you may want to take a look at some of these readings instead of the more generic ones elsewhere in this guide.

This section includes readings for Advent/Christmas, Lent, Holy Week, and Easter. There is also a reading here for the first day of Autumn and one for the U.S. Fourth of July.

Do you have a favorite holiday? A least favorite one?

Why not write your own devotional about a holiday – Halloween, Dia de los Muertos, Winter Solstice, Pride Week, the first day of Spring, and so on?

The First Day of Autumn

On a walk around my neighborhood on the first day of autumn, and just for fun, I looked for browns and oranges (they're not my favorite colors, but I've come to appreciate them).

Brown: The tips of the iris leaves, curling parchment, their blossoms long gone, pine cones by the side of the road, just one or two. Nowhere near their tree. And the autumn grass of lawns, browning in the sun.

Orange: The painted strip on the "road closed" signs all around the neighborhood (we were getting repaved, you see). The "fiber optic" poles planted alongside the road and small flags indicating where city crews should – or should not – dig. Periodically, there were the school's yard signs proclaiming "future leader lives here." I saw, too, the bright leash of the gorgeous black lab on its daily walk with its human. And, yes, the pumpkins, a few marigolds, and the tiny blossoms of an unknown flower. But mostly it was urban orange.

I am a bit jealous of those poets who live in the woods or by the ocean, and write such beautiful things, and see such glory in the sunsets and surprise wildlife encounters.

I live in a city that I love. And we have repaving instead of elk (although we do have raccoons, squirrels, maybe a fox, and a rabbit or two, which explains the fox). And the smell of asphalt.

And the sounds of highway traffic, which, under certain conditions, *could* sound like waves breaking on the shore, if you ignore the horns.

Urban orange. And the browning grass.

I was hoping for the turning of leaves, the brown crunching of them underfoot. What I got was urban orange, yet discovered therein signs of life, of repairing, making, moving.

And the brown of the spent grass, not indicating the ending of things, but rather a good long rest before beginning again.

Ongoing Reflection Questions, Suggestions, and/or Things to Think About

- Make a pact with yourself for the first day (or thereabouts) of autumn, of spring, of summer AND of winter, to go outside and move around your neighborhood as you are able. Take special note of the colors of each season, at the variety of colors in each season. Even if it's only white, or brown – look at all the shades of white and brown. What is going on in the neighborhood, what are the sounds of each season? Marvel and wonder at the diversity that you see as you move around.

- What season are you in at this moment? It will change, of course, but what season are you in now? If you're old-ish (like me), that doesn't necessarily mean you are in the autumn or winter of your life, either. Just sayin'.

- Based on this reading and your own reflections, do any scripture passages come to mind? These can be scriptures from a variety of religious traditions.

Deep Into the Dark

Christmas is
  contradiction and wonder
  soft candle-light and fear

Christmas goes deep into the dark, yet we search for it in glitter,
  and we decorate with tinsel the tears of
    those left behind
    those left out
    those left alone.

Christmas goes deep into the dark to meet us there;
  deep into the dark to touch with power those left behind, those
      left out, those left alone

Christmas is where points of pain meet, yet are met with something
      of life,

Christmas is raising a candle together in the dark, daring to sing of
      love.

Christmas taps us on the shoulder with a shepherd's crook,
  and we begin to smell the sheep,
  and the unwashed bodies of their keepers who
    simply say, "Come with us,.."
They're the ones who really know the way to Bethlehem:
  Where lament and possibility intertwine, not destroying each
      other,
    but listening.
  Where love and loss sit side by side,
    like two old people on a park bench,
      one occasionally resting their head on the other's shoulder.

Because Christmas is not an ethereal "making everything alright"
      sort of holiday
  but it finds its home in the dirt and the blood and the sinew of
      each of us.

Christmas is
  warmth and cold
  light and dark

joy and pain
work and rest
mystery and surprise

But always a presence
  of something holy
  of community
  of dancers in the dark
  of candlelight's defiance, power, and hope
  of laughter and song
  of you, of me
    and the sacred spaces between and among and within us.

Ongoing Reflection Questions, Suggestions, and/or Things to Think About

- How are you this Advent season? Where is Christmas meeting you?

- Try to get in touch with someone for whom Christmas is going to be hard this year – someone who has suffered a loss (of friend or family or pet or job or health), or who is alone, or struggling emotionally or with addiction issues, or with transitions in their life. You can be that "something of life" that meets them at their points of pain. (I am an Introvert, so I sympathize if you find this hard to do).

- If the holidays are hard for you this year (or maybe every year), stop and take a breath. You will get through it. This poem is for you especially. The Holy One, that force of love on which all Creation is based, comes to those points of pain. You are the one for whom this story was written.

- Based on this reading and your own reflections, do any scripture passages come to mind? These can be scriptures from a variety of religious traditions.

A Christmas Poem from THE DOGS

Christmas cookies, Christmas treats
World's best moms that can't be beat!
These are presents we adore,
Every day and evermore!

We can't write poems, but hey, we try,
When we're apart it makes us cry,
We know you love us and we love you
   (So where's dinner?)
With wagging tails and hearts so true!

Merry Christmas, Moms, we say,
Who walk us, feed us, and with us play.
We love you more than we can say
So we'll slobber on you every day
And you can't make us go away
And we don't really know how to stop this poem…..
But that's ok. ♥♥♥♥♥♥♥

Ongoing Reflection Questions, Suggestions, and/or Things to Think About

- I wrote this alleged poem for some dear friends and their two lovely Golden Retrievers. It's simply a silly piece (my friends liked it, though!). "Doggerel" if you will (groan).

- Wherever you are in progressing through this devotional guide, or wherever you are in your life, I figure you could use a laugh right about now. A break, as it were, from intensity.

- Because that's the way the world seems so much of the time. It seems like our world so often is in an "I could really use a laugh right about now" state.

- So go ahead. Let yourself chuckle (or groan) at this silly poem. Enjoy! And realize that regardless of the state of the world, there are also spaces of and for grace, laughter, and even some (good) silliness.

- And go ahead – write your own silly poem! They are surprisingly easy to write. So write something silly. You might be surprised at what other creativity may emerge.

- And, just for fun, I'll even ask the question I always ask with these devotional readings: Based on this reading and your own reflections, do any scripture passages come to mind? These can be scriptures from a variety of religious traditions. It would be fascinating to see what you may come up with!

On What I Know and Don't Know About Christmas

Day One

Driving in the neighborhood one afternoon in December, I saw a car sporting a bright red nose, reindeer antlers sprouting from each of the side front windows. It made me smile to think of that driver moving through the season in a giant reindeer.

By Northern Hemisphere reckoning, Christmastime is the darkest time of the year. And cold, in most areas. It made me smile to remember that in the darkness of time and history, there is still playfulness. I don't know what "spirit of Christmas" the driver was trying to impart. But I do know I was caught by that spell of play and humor.

A light shines in the darkness, and sometimes it makes us laugh.

I don't always know what to make of this holiday season. But I do know there is something holy, some power, some force – love, if you will – that has entered our world of messiness, violence, grief, injustice. It has always been there but we needed reminding.

I do know that love – the core of Christmas – is light that shines in the gloom, proclamation and reminder that the gloom will not overcome it.

A thought: *What shines for you during this season? And how are you a light for others?*

Day Two

Love is the core of Christmas. It is a light that shines in the darkness, proclaiming and reminding that the darkness will not overcome it.

And I have watched the core of Christmas emerge in surprising ways:

- At the funeral home late in the afternoon, I watched as two brothers walked together to the casket; the younger could just barely see over its rim. I watched as the older brother stood with the younger, and gently stroked his back and talked quietly to him as they looked upon their mother. Did they gather at a sort of manger? One birthing grief, gentleness, and love in the face of loss. And a light shone in the darkness.

- At a funeral reception once, I watched as the family, who had repeatedly been touched by tragedy, laughed and danced, tripping over each other, singing as they danced. Life reasserting itself. Community of shared pain, memory, joy. Tears never far, emptiness just at the edges, but the light shone in the darkness.

- At another time and place, in the nursing home, I watched a parishioner as she sat beside her husband of sixty years, gently talking to him as he lay there, agitated yet unresponsive. I watched as she gave him the Communion I had brought, dipping a small sponge into the grape juice, tenderly moving it around the inside of his mouth. I watched as he calmed and rested, the sacrament embracing his ravaged brain. Had he tasted the angels' "Fear not"?

A thought: You are loved. Just know that. And, you can be that core of Christmas for others.

Day Three

I may not know a lot of things, but I do know that Christmas is about something truly grand, and that it fights against all that would tear creation apart.

And I know it takes our participation for that to happen. No *Deus ex machina*, this, but a young woman giving birth on a cold night in a barn, with poor and dispossessed shepherds the bearers of the good news.

It's an older brother helping a little boy navigate grief, an old woman's sacramental touch, and a grieving family with the courageous audacity to dance.

I've watched
  love and loss
  community and hope
  courage and compassion
  pain and laughter
  life moving in and through
  love holding tight and letting go

I've watched and witnessed – with the shepherds and the animals – the core of Christmas unfolding, settling in, taking root.

A thought: *You have it within you to participate in this "something truly grand," through your own unique gifts and ways of being, through ordinary acts and courageous witness.*

Ongoing Reflection Questions, Suggestions, and/or Things to Think About

- What are your stories of light shining in the gloom? Of hope where you thought there was none? Of dancing through the tears?

- If someone – some critter or person, or landscape or star or river (you get my drift...) – has shone for you and helped you dance with hope, and find life – let them know in some way, the gift they have been for you. If they are no longer with you, imagine a conversation with the person or the pup or the mountain, and celebrate that gift.

- How can you be a gift to Creation? How can you help endangered species find life, bleached coral reefs find healing, dry riverbeds find hope? Endangered peoples, disappeared peoples, grieving peoples – how can you be part of the endeavors for justice, healing, accountability, joy? Everyone can have a place in this good work.

- Based on this reading and your own reflections, do any scripture passages (other than the obvious Christmas ones) come to mind? These can be scriptures from a variety of religious traditions.

135

Nativity Seen

In haiku form

The Burro
I carried Mary
to a manger of questions:
Now what? Why this? And?

The Sheep
They woke us from sleep:
Angel lights and shouts and song.
Wondering, we came.

The Rat
(You never see me –
The rat in the manger scene.
I'm sure I was there.)

The Dog
Of course there's a dog!
Ubiquitous dog – that's me!
Sanctified warmth, love.

The Cat
Naturally, a cat.
Dignified, aloof, I am,
With curious awe.

And so
We all shoved for space,
for warmth, and comfort, and glimpse
of strange miracles.

Ongoing Reflection Questions, Suggestions, and/or Things to Think About

- Do you have a Nativity set in your house? We add things to ours each year – a llama, a couple of moose, a badger, and so on. Why not? Our Magi progress around the living room during Advent, accompanied by one of the moose, who keeps them in line. They eventually make it to the table where the rest of the Nativity scene is, just in time for Christmas Eve. (Yeah, I know, that's not theologically correct – they came later. But I suspect moose, a badger, and a llama aren't theologically correct, either, and they appear every year anyway.)

- So, go ahead – play with your Nativity set! Move things around. Create back-stories for the characters. Get involved with the scene and perhaps you may discover some "strange miracles" as you engage with this story. At the very least, you might have some fun.

- Based on this reading and your own reflections, do any scripture passages come to mind? These can be scriptures from a variety of religious traditions.

A Lenten Prayer: I Have a Few Questions

(Adapted from a larger Lenten service "Lent: a Journey from Separation to Community", which can be found on https://allyson.revsawtell.org/)

Here I am, God, in this quiet time and place, on holy ground......and, God, I have a few questions.

This journey of Lent, with so much separation within me, my community, and our world, is like a sprawling, eternal abyss. We all gather at the edge, looking out across the expanse and wonder......how in your holy name will we get to the other side?

How can I do this hard work to help to bring your new world into being? How can I continue to live with lament and with hope and with celebration, too?

Help me confront this abyss of separation from myself, from others, and from all Creation. Help me get down in the depths and, with others, to find a way across.

O God, with you all things are possible. And within our communities of faith and of common purpose, a lot of things are possible!

Together, we will find a way. Help us live like we believe it! Grant us courage, grant us wisdom.

For the love of your Creation. Amen!

Ongoing Reflection Questions, Suggestions, and/or Things to Think About

- This reading moves from "I" to "we". Even if you pray this in solitude, remember you are still part of the wider community of humans, the wider community of all Creation.

- Who are the communities that give you courage and hope? Family? Friends? Pods of whales, herds of bison, mountain ranges, forests? All of those – and more – are communities that can give life and to whom we are connected.

- Create a small altar of pictures and symbols of those communities. This can simply be a small table, or part of your desk, on which you put photos, stuffed animals, little statues – anything that reminds you of your beloved communities.

- If you don't feel you have a community to which you can relate, and that can support you and give you hope, try, try to find one. Whether it comes from volunteering in your community, or joining an online group (a support group, or a game-playing group, for example), try to see if you can find one. We are meant to be in relationship, and you are worthy of that love and support.

- Based on this reading and your own reflections, do any scripture passages come to mind? These can be scriptures from a variety of religious traditions.

The Arms of Love

Lent is a journey we go through together in community. Sometimes we're making it up as we go along, sometimes we lean heavily on our traditions and history, sometimes we create new ways out of the old.

But how do we do this work of lament, longing, hope, justice and joy? How can we as individuals and even as a church, make any difference in our battered world?

Begin by remembering that you are held in the arms of Love always.

And then you become the arms of love for another, who becomes the arms of love for yet another, and another.

And on it goes.

In your work, your prayers, your tears and your laughter, on it goes. In your everyday lives, on it goes.

As you open your heart to Creation's devastation and work to restore our world, you become the arms of love for earth, air, sky, water, plant, animal, mineral.

And on it goes.

This is who we are – arms of love embracing a devastated world.

We may have forgotten. We may be too overwhelmed to even think about this.

But this is who we are!

Not isolated, but a community of life trying its best to restore and repair, to bring together, to hold accountable, to heal, and to transform.

This is who we are and what we are called to do.

God help us, and push us, and hold us for the sake of your Creation, O Holy One.

Amen!

Ongoing Reflection Questions, Suggestions, and/or Things to Think About

- Give yourself a hug. Be the arms of love for yourself.

- Create an altar, or a space on your desk or table, and put pictures or symbols there of those people/creatures/other parts of Creation for whom you could be "arms of love" from your one space, with your one life. Then move beyond "thoughts and prayers" and find some sort of action: volunteer in an animal shelter or a food bank, donate blood or platelets at your local hospital, march at Pridefest, testify at your state house, energy regulatory commission, or school board hearings about issues dear to your heart.

- Based on this reading and your own reflections, do any scripture passages come to mind? These can be scriptures from a variety of religious traditions.

Tomb-Time

A reading for Good Friday

Flowers peeking out in early spring's warm sun
    Then comes frost and snow
Flowers, minus some greenery, again peeking out in late spring
    Oh look – a hailstorm
In the aftermath – eventually, surprisingly – some return and begin
    to bud.

The question is, at what point will they not come back?

What happens when hope dies, and the light goes out in your heart?

Creation's hope is dying; the light is fading from the heart of all life.

Humanity's ongoing desecration of Creation, and our clinging to
    Business as Usual, seal us into death.

This is where words stop, logic fails, and nothing makes sense.

Let it go. Lie down in the cold and dark for a time.

All that is disappearing is worthy of this grief.

This is tomb-time.

[Sit in silence for a while]

And then (and this is important), hold on, however feebly, to the
memory of a story that says the tomb is not the end. The stone is
rolled away by people and communities of hope and hard work. You
can join them in this work, and emerge into life again.

Ongoing Reflection Questions, Suggestions, and/or Things to Think About

- What is happening to our world – its creatures, people, climate, air, water, forests and oceans – is devastating to contemplate and to witness and to feel the repercussions of. But the more you are involved in trying to make change, the less helpless you may feel. Here are some things you can do (if you haven't already done so):

  o Try to find a Climate Grief group near where you live, or where you can access through Zoom. Join it.

  o Look for groups that work in the areas of environmental justice and restoration of Creation. Join them. Or get on their mailing list (I know, another email. Ick). Again, you may already be doing this.

  o Look into Our Children's Trust (https://www.ourchildrenstrust.org/), or Fridays for Future (https://fridaysforfuture.org/), or Sunrise Movement (https://www.sunrisemovement.org/ – all are movements led by youth and children and their adult allies, and they have been remarkably effective. They are places of hope.

- Based on this reading and your own reflections, do any scripture passages come to mind? These can be scriptures from a variety of religious traditions.

The Cry of Christ

A reading for the Christian tradition of Holy Week

The cry of Christ is the cry of Creation.

And when Creation cries out in pain, rage and sorrow, whose voice is it?

The One born of Mary, proclaiming the reversing of things, and the tumbling of empires.

The One who ran the money changers out of the Temple, enraged at their exploitation of the vulnerable and voiceless. (Let those who have ears, hear!)

When Creation cries out in pain, rage and sorrow, whose voice is it? Christ of the cross, whose death at the hands of greed, apathy, fear, and Business as Usual, invalidated those same powers.

It is also the voice of the Risen One:
The Risen Christ, bearing memories, scars, wounds and wonder.
The Christ of cup and bread, of calling out into community and power.
The One who calls Creation to rise again.

And now we are the pierced hands that see to that work.

Ongoing Reflection Questions, Suggestions, and/or Things to Think About

- Where do you hear the "cry of Christ"?

- Based on this reading and your own reflections, do any other scripture passages come to mind? These can be scriptures from a variety of religious traditions.

An Absurd Reading for Easter:
Lather, Rinse, Repeat

Doesn't it strike you as odd, those open-ended instructions on the shampoo bottle that say "Lather – Rinse – Repeat"? For how long? When do you stop? It's like not being able to stop spelling "banana"!

"Lather – Rinse – Repeat." Our imaginative selves conjure a vision of some poor soul in an unending cycle of shampooing and rinsing, over and over, until their hair falls out.

Our rational selves chuckle and say "Oh for heaven's sake! It's obvious – repeat once, of course!" Absurd to think otherwise.

Our imaginative selves – who appreciate the absurd – wonder about it anyway. We ask those questions that may sound ridiculous, because our imaginative selves don't think the answer is obvious at all.

Easter is that time of celebrating the absurd: What?! Life overcomes death?! Proclaiming, celebrating this absurdity. And then doing it.

Easter is a "Lather – Rinse – Repeat" phenomenon and it doesn't end:

> Celebrate (our beloved Creation)
> Acknowledge and lament our separation from it and our
> participation in causing its pain.
> Reach out to each other and all the web of life.
> Embody hope and don't give up (or, at least not often).

And do that all over again. And again. And again.

Celebrate joyously on Easter that life is triumphant. Then, leap back into the fray.

Because we must, and because we can. And because that's where life and beloved community reside.

So on Easter we celebrate! And then jump back into the hard stuff. Together.

Ongoing Reflection Questions, Suggestions, and/or Things to Think About

- Go ahead, get some chocolate. Or some jelly beans (The black ones are my favorites. What's yours?). Gather together your favorite items and your favorite people that help you celebrate. It doesn't have to be on Easter, either. Just plan a celebration with special people and/or special critters. Celebrate life and love – they really do triumph over all that other s#*t that tries to nail us and throw us in the tomb.

- Oh, and wash your hair before the big party. And don't forget to lather – rinse – repeat.

- Based on this reading and your own reflections, do any scripture passages come to mind? These can be scriptures from a variety of religious traditions.

The Journey Leads Us To An Empty Tomb

(If you're expecting answers, you need to sing another song)

The journey leads us to an empty tomb
  Easter brings surprise
  Easter brings a shout and a sob

The journey leads us to an empty tomb
  Easter brings questions
    Who are we? Who are we to become? What do we do now?
Where do we go from here?

The journey leads us to an empty tomb
    A beginning, not an ending
    Life triumphs, life flourishes!

  God picks us up, spins us around, and pushes us out, saying "Go!
Love! Hope!"
    And "When did I say it would be easy?"
    And "Do you really think you're alone?"

The journey leads us – together – to an empty tomb.

Whatever happened then touches us now.
  We are the body of Christ
  We are called to embody God's love by what we do and who we
are
    To hope and not give up
    To keep striving to heal all creation
    To reach out and transform separation to connection
    To build the beloved community and fight despair
    To confront, challenge, and struggle with all that would destroy
and demean.

And not forget to laugh.

The journey leads us to an empty tomb.
  Easter is celebration and call, resistance and question, laughter and
surprise.
  Easter is hope.

We came to the tomb expecting duty and grief
  And we found
    Mystery, space, questions, joy, hope

Today, tomorrow, and always.

Ongoing Reflection Questions, Suggestions, and/or Things to Think About

- Laugh today! Enjoy that chocolate Easter bunny and those jelly beans! May spring come into your soul and your heart. May warmth and joy be yours, even as you struggle, and even as you keep working to help heal our beloved Creation.

- Based on this reading and your own reflections, do any scripture passages come to mind? These can be scriptures from a variety of religious traditions.

What Was Seen Instead

Looking out the window as my train moved through the prairielands
   I searched for the cranes in migration

But saw instead
  A large human-sized white and pink stuffed Easter rabbit,
  Sitting at a table on a front porch.
  One ear stirred in the spring breeze.

Then we moved on by.
Still no cranes. Or antelope. Or deer.

Instead, just a large Easter rabbit,
   staring amiably at the passing train.
I kept waiting for it to wave.
It might have.

Ongoing Reflection Questions, Suggestions, and/or Things to Think About

- Easter is a time of reveling in the unexpected good news of life triumphant. Revel away! Celebrate life wherever you find it. May unexpected goodness and joy be yours! And may you be a contributor to someone else's good news and joy! And to Creation's good news and joy!

- And while you're at it, find time for whimsy, humor, and wonder-struck laughter.

- Based on this reading and your own reflections, do any scripture passages (other than the obvious Easter ones) come to mind? These can be scriptures from a variety of religious traditions.

Fourth of July Weekend, 2022

Birdsong emerged over the roar of the motorcycle outside my window. Persistent, it made itself heard.

Sometimes, loving my country is like trying to love a spouse or a child who is a meth addict, with the wasting away, the anger and rage, the damage, the deceit.

Where is birdsong in the torn and shredded nature of it all?

Sometimes I wish the birdsong would be swallowed up in the noise, and I could be lulled to sleep by the motorcycle's lullaby.

Yet, I heard birdsong faintly over the roar of the motorcycle.

Still, I heard birdsong.

Ongoing Reflection Questions, Suggestions, and/or Things to Think About

- What is it like for you to relate to your country? Do you feel you have a country?

- Where are those times when you just wanted to give in to the status quo and to stop fighting and working for a new and better world? To just be lulled to sleep by Business as Usual? Let somebody else fight those battles for justice and for healing of Creation. Sometimes it's OK to step back for a bit from the struggle, to take a breath, to rest. But always with the intent of getting back into the fray.

- A friend told me once (and she was paraphrasing someone, she couldn't remember who) that when faced with something hard or challenging, you could "borrow courage from your future self. The self that already did that hard thing and made it through." Imagine your future self, talking to you. What are they saying to you?

- Based on this reading and your own reflections, do any scripture passages come to mind? These can be scriptures from a variety of religious traditions.

Sending Forth

You can save these readings for when you are completely finished with the entire devotional guide, if you wish.

Another option is to pick one to reflect on when you need a benediction or a sending forth, as you set out to do something new or daunting. If you need a blessing, a challenge or a charge, read these.

Just sit with them, breathe them in. Know that you are beloved, blessed, and called forth.

Carve Out Hope

Have you ever seen those intricately fashioned pieces of jewelry, carved from the found antlers of moose, deer, elk?

From a living creature that followed its own internal signals for growth and change, shedding an exquisite piece of itself, which someone else transformed into beauty of another sort.

Carve out hope like that:
    Find the pieces of life and beauty hidden in the undergrowth
    What was forgotten and left behind is re-membered again, in a
        new way.
Carve out hope.

What does it look like?
    Something precious and alive held in your hands, what it might
        become still unknown.

But it's the holding that counts. Solid in your hands, not to slip between your fingers to shatter on the hard ground, or to be lost and trampled over in the undergrowth. But something real.

Carve out hope.
Hold it in your hands. Feel its texture, and dream of what it might become.

And then, offer it to another, half-made because you cannot form it all yourself, yet still real and of value.

Carve out hope from what you find around you. A thing of beauty even in the hands of an amateur artisan – for aren't we all – a thing of beauty precisely for its awkward angles, rough edges, and "interesting" design.

Carve out hope. Not alone. What is real and true is what we discover
        or just stumble upon
through hard work or simple surprise, and what we make of it
        together.

Carve out hope. And you are changed in the making.

Not Ordinary Times

These are not ordinary times
    We hide from the "not"
    We cling to the "ordinary" in our little boxes, calmly adjusting our blinders,
Shaking our heads at these times.

But a pit opens up in our stomach
    The sense of something not right settles in our bones
    A "yes, but…" sits uneasily in our souls and gnaws and nags
And a grief too heavy to bear chokes us like summer wildfire,
    Hot and violent
    Embers scorching all we know.

A suspicion grows in us that if we
    Embrace the "yes, but"
    And peer into the pit,
A way may be found.
Or a hope of a possibility of a way
    May be found
And a hole might be burned through our little boxes of protection,
    Releasing the toxic gases of denial and despair
    Dissipating into the clear cold air
    Transforming to hope and hard work.

These are not ordinary times.
    Yet we wave it away,
      ("Can't happen to us…"
        Sea levels won't reach *our* mountaintop")
    And in ignorance, or desperation, or simple greed, we make the "over" the ordinary
      Overfishing
      Overcrowding
      Overgrazing

Overconsuming
Overwhelming loss and devastation

But a pit opens up in our stomach.
Subterranean fear gnaws,
        Chewing holes in our denial.
"Something is not right" echoes in our souls:
  The cry of Creation
    The voice of God.

"These are not ordinary times"
  may be the path towards our resurrection.

So we bathe in courage, grasp for community
  Leave the shelter of business-as-usual
And stare into the face of this unknown future.
We leave our little boxes and cast off our blinders
  And the bright light of Creation's pain nearly blinds us
  And grief nearly chokes us.

But not quite.

Because when there's enough of us stumbling around,
  trying to make a way,
Sooner or later we'll begin to connect,
  And the power of that connection explodes in hope
  And a different way can be made
  And life can flourish in new and extraordinary ways.

Do you believe? Do you dare?

The Pledge

To the mourning dove outside the window,
And to the song;

To the humpback whale leaping from the cold Alaska
waters;
To the earthworm digging in the soil, bringing in air and life,
  and occasionally feeding the persistent robin;

To the wolves, coyotes and bears,
Who by their very nature bring
Eco-systems into balance;

To the bee on the dandelion, nourished and nourishing
others;
To the salmon pushing upstream to spawn and die,
  That uphill battle for life, the giving of itself for the sake
of the future;

To these, and all wild creatures, I pledge...

No.

I *pray*:
  In gratitude and with joy for their part and presence in the
web of life;
  For forgiveness for the threat we humans bring, the
damage we are doing,
  and for the disruption we cause.

I *pray*
  For the courage to
      seek
      learn
      commit
      and fight
  For the sake of all wild life
  For the sake of God's good Creation

And for the whole web of life which we share with all wild creatures.

I pray, and lament,
I pray, and dance with joy.

I stand in awe and wonder,
And wonder what the future holds.

And so I pray
  For courage and focus,
  For strength and compassion.

That I may begin to fashion that future where we all work together to mend and spin our web of life. May this be so. Amen!

People of Hope

Hope is that sure and certain knowledge that we may not know always what's coming next, but we know what we are pulled towards: the Beloved Community of justice and accountability, of the mending and tending of Creation, of connectedness and joy.

Be that hope! Live that hope! In community.

And may the love of God, the power of your community of faith, and the embrace of the whole community of Creation, permeate your very being, now and always.

Amen!

Photographs

All photos (unless otherwise indicated) were taken by Allyson, on her cell phone. They include:

- From "A Blessing for the Earth" – Canyonlands Needles District, near Moab Utah, October 2018

- From "Deep Peace" – Sunset over the Pacific Ocean, Washington Coast, September 2022

- From "Holy Distraction, Batman!" – Sunrise outside my front window, Denver, January 2012

- From "Reflections on Mary Oliver's *Wild Geese* – Rio Grande Gorge, outside of Taos, New Mexico, August 2016

- From "Two Domes" – taken from outside the front of Union Station, Washington DC; April 2022

- From "Just Stop" – Sunset over Denver, June 2018

- From "Blessing of our Animal Companions" – My dog friends Riley and Chevy Lou, August 2019

- From "Wolves" – Prairie Dogs, Cherry Creek State Park, Aurora, Colorado 2022 (Taken by Peter Sawtell)

- From "Prayer of Thanksgiving for the Wild Creatures" – Grey Jay, Yellowstone National Park Wyoming, August 2021

- From "Blessing of the Wild Ones" – Bald Eagle, in Denver's Washington Park, February 2023

- From "The First Day of Autumn" – in the Corn Maze at Denver Botanic Gardens, Chatfield *(technically not in my neighborhood, as I mentioned in the poem; just a bit of poetic license, here!)*

- From "Nativity Seen" – a homemade Nativity scene, made many years ago by my very creative sister-in-law (with a few added critters of our own).

- Back Cover – photo taken at the 2019 Global Climate Strike, Denver. (Taken on Allyson's cell phone by another march participant)

www.ingramcontent.com/pod-product-compliance
Lightning Source LLC
Chambersburg PA
CBHW051525120626
46551CB00012B/1080